Sins of the Son

CARLTON STOWERS

NEW YORK

sins
of the
son

The names of certain individuals appearing in this book have been changed to protect their privacy.

For information address: Hyperion, 114 Fifth Avenue, New York, New York 10011.

LIBRARY OF CONGRESS CATALOGING-IN-PUBLICATION DATA

Stowers, Carlton.

Sins of the son / by Carlton Stowers.—1st ed.

p. cm.

ISBN 0-7868-6091-X

1. Stowers, Anson, 1963——Family. 2. Murderers—Texas— Biography. 3. Uxoricide—Texas. 4. Wife abuse—Texas. 5. Stowers, Carlton—Family. 6. Fathers—Texas—Psychology. 7. Fathers and sons—Texas. I. Title.

HV6248.S635S76 1995

364.1′523′092—dc20

[B] 95-2636

CIP

Design by Beth Tondreau Design

FIRST EDITION

10   9   8   7   6   5   4   3   2

To all fathers and sons

In the middle of the journey of our life
I found myself in a dark wood,
For I had lost the right path.
> —Dante, *Inferno*

. . . with rejection comes anger, and with anger
some kind of crime in revenge for the rejection,
and with the crime guilt—and there is the
story of mankind.
> —John Steinbeck, *East of Eden*

Preface

IT IS TRADITION, I understand, to use these introductory pages to gently tease the reader's interest, dropping a few well-placed hints that provide some idea of what one's book is about. In this case, however, I think it more important to point out what this book *is not*. It is neither an apology nor a manipulative exercise of literary sympathy-seeking. It is, simply, a story of the lives of two people—my son and me—who have traveled a bumpy, sometimes misdirected thirty-year course marked by the ordinary and extraordinary. That it seeks answers is obvious; but there is no promise that all questions have been neatly resolved.

Nor have I attempted clarifying social and psychological observations I'm woefully unqualified to make. At best, putting the story to paper has provided me some understanding, some logical sorting of things that have benefitted me and, I hope, might be of some aid to others.

Which is to say this project was born of admittedly selfish, cathartic intent.

There will, I know, be critics quick to label what I've done an exploitation. They are fully entitled to their opinion. My only response is that this is a project that has played on my mind for many years, a private muse that, in time, literally begged for public airing. Yet even after making the commitment to its writing following long discussions with my son about direction and purpose, there were times of doubt. More than once during the course of telling this story, I considered abandoning it for a more comfortable subject. Yet I found myself continuing to press on, reflecting and writing. The book, quite literally, kept calling out to me.

Why? Because I felt the need to see where the story went, what too-long-hidden truths might, in fact, be discovered.

When, some time ago, while enjoying the warm afternoon sun in a prison yard, my son asked what had prompted my desire to write such a book, my response was not immediate despite the fact it was a question deserving an honest reply. I rose from the bench where we were seated, went inside for a cup of bitter vending machine coffee, then returned to where he waited.

I did not, I finally explained, want to go to my grave wondering what had happened to us, not having made the effort to understand why our relationship had been what it was. I needed to know how love and anger could so long coexist between two people. I needed to know the reasons for his behavior and the degree of blame I should rightfully bear. It was time for straight-forward answers, painful though they might be.

Too, there seemed to me an issue of fair play to consider.

In recent years, I have focused a great deal of my professional attention on books and articles that deal with crimes and the deep, painful scars they leave. I've spent agonizing hours in the company of grieving mothers and fathers, husbands and wives, friends and family, who, in complete trust, have detailed for me their most intimate thoughts. I shared the lives of the families of three bright and talented teenagers who were brutally murdered during an innocent trip to a lake near Waco, Texas, there to do nothing more than sit on a park bench and watch what would ultimately become their final sunset. The parents of a twenty-one-year-old undercover narcotics officer, murdered by the teenage son of a Dallas police officer, welcomed me into their home and tearfully described the nightmare their lives had become. My sympathy for them was great, but no more so than that I would come to feel for the caring, heartbroken parents of the misguided youngster who had pulled the trigger, then gone off to spend years behind prison bars.

I've heard the wrenching story of a mother whose daughter left one evening to attend a concert, never to be heard from again; spent long, into-the-night hours with a distraught husband falsely accused of the torturous murder of his estranged wife; listened to the terrifying recollections of those who saw loved ones randomly gunned down when a deranged young man named George Hennard entered a Luby's cafeteria in Killeen, Texas, and began randomly taking lives in a fit of madness; came to know residents of a strange religious commune who called themselves Branch Davidians and felt a horror and outrage that will haunt me forever as their lives and those of their innocent children were lost in an inferno watched by television viewers around the world.

Throughout such interviews, there has been a recurring theme: a generous candor, regardless of pain and sorrow, from those with whom I have spoken.

In return, I cannot do less.

Introduction

PARENTHOOD IS TERROR, if we allow ourselves to consider the possibilities.

A life sentence of sleep deprivation, listening for the door to open, holding the breath. Biting the tongue.

Punishment imposed for the crime of loving.

How many of us with children have knocked wood when the fever abates or the croup clears or the blood test comes back normal? How many have relinquished the car keys with jaws clenched to the point of tetany, fighting back gorefest imagery as we mouth the requisite "Have a good time; be careful"?

How many have rationalized personal misfortune with "As long as the kids are healthy"? Chuckled at the bumper sticker "Insanity is genetic. You inherit it from your kids," knowing deep down it's *profound*?

How many have discovered or rediscovered prayer?

Please God, keep them safe.

Dear Lord, don't let them be victims.

Bacon was at his most insightful when he called children "hostages to fortune."

But what of the parent whose child becomes the hostage taker?

I FIRST BECAME aware of Carlton Stowers's work several years ago when I read his true-crime masterpiece and eventual Edgar winner, *Careless Whispers*. The book chronicled the relentless struggle of an obscure Texas sheriff to solve the murders of a group of teenagers. A good man up against baffling, apparently senseless crimes, venturing where no one else gave a damn. Perfect story for a crime reporter, but Stowers was so much more than yet another journalist milking tabloid lust.

The book made a huge impression on me because Carlton's writing was beautiful, his pacing flawless, his ability to characterize through nuance reminiscent of our best novelists. Perhaps most important of all, he exhibited that special sensitivity and gift for creating intimacy with victims and their families unique to the finest practitioners of the genre.

All the while, he was grappling with the psychological and social deterioration of his firstborn son, Anson, a hellish descent that culminated in senseless homicide.

I won't insult your intelligence by going on about irony or Greek tragedy, or pontificating about more than one kind of victimization. Nor will I hold out the promise of solutions to cosmic conundrums within the pages of this book.

What *Sins of the Son* will do is immerse you in a heartbreaking and courageous and compulsively readable story devoid of self-pity or pat theories. A remarkably honest, sometimes cold-eyed account of a special kind of parental terror wrought by one of our finest crime writers out of the depths of his own nightmare.

Sins of the Son is that rarity in the age of hype: a *truly* unforgettable tale that will remain with you long after you've turned the last page.

—Jonathan Kellerman

Sins of the Son

As the door draws closed
   The cloak of darkness does descend.
      Final pictures now are posed,
         Holding hopes we must pretend.
And the life we chose has reached its end.

Every day another test,
   As life spins slowly past,
      An ordeal suffered without rest.
         A great and numbing mental fast.
            A flowing wave without crest.
Descending darkness shall ever last.

The silent ticking of the clock,
   Reminding of the time that's lost.
      A single glance will show the lock,
         The icy wall sheathed in frost,
            Barren ground of solid rock.
To this end that fine line was crossed.
                  —Anson Stowers, "Lost," 1993

One

THE VOICES OF chil-
dren were still singing a
quiet, pleasant tune in my head
as I drove toward home on that sunny, unseasonably mild
November afternoon in 1988. It had been something called
National Book Week, and along with most other authors in the
community, I had been invited to visit one of the Dallas elementary schools to spend some time reading to and talking with the
students. With the holiday season fast approaching, I had chosen
to read from Chris Van Allsburg's lyrical children's fantasy *The*

Polar Express, and the students had loved it. They had sat in rapt silence, listening to the story of a trainload of youngsters swept away on a magical journey to the North Pole, then *oohed* and *ahhed* at the author's magnificent illustrations, which I had passed among them. Afterward, there had been cookies and punch and a considerable amount of enthusiastic discussion of the story they'd just heard.

It had, then, been a pleasant experience. Not only had it provided me a brief respite from deadline concerns over a book I was struggling to complete, but it also had been time I judged well spent. I drove from the parking lot of Winnetka Elementary School, warmed by the friendly smiles and applause of my young audience.

In no real hurry to get home, I detoured past a fast-food restaurant for a cup of coffee to wash away the saccharine taste of the Kool-Aid punch and idly read a newspaper discarded by some member of the lunch crowd. An electrical fire, triggered by the previous evening's violent thunderstorm, had thrown thousands of downtown workers into darkness for a few hours. There was mixed reaction to the police chief's announcement that he was promoting three blacks, an Hispanic, and a woman. President Bush was busy assembling an economics team he hoped could do something about reducing the federal deficit, a teenage mother had been charged with trying to sell her newborn baby for $550, and the Pistons had defeated the Dallas Mavericks by fifteen.

The headlines made little impression, blurred by the still fresh thoughts of the children I'd just visited and the memories the occasion had suddenly renewed.

How many years had passed since those times when I had read

bedtime fairy tales to my own kids, sneaking peeks from the pages to watch as their eyelids fluttered in a vain attempt to remain open until the story's end? How long had it been since those days of quicksilver childhood innocence when the lines between fantasy and reality were still comfortably blurred and Santa and his North Pole toy shop were real?

And how was I to know that the bright warmth of that day was soon to turn cold and pitch black?

Life offers no weightier chore than that of being the bearer of another's bad news. The burden, prompted by a phone call from a police dispatcher an hour earlier, marked my wife's face as she met me at the door. The ever present sparkle was gone from her eyes, replaced by a lost, dull sadness. She had, I could tell, been crying.

I felt a sudden rush of anxiety as she moved toward me and put her arms around my neck, burying her face against my collarbone.

"What?"

"It's Anson," she finally said, her words forced with a dread I'd never before heard. Though not the mother of my son, she knew firsthand of our troubled relationship. "He's in the county jail. I was so afraid you would hear about it on the radio. I'm sorry . . . so sorry."

In what could only have been a split second, I mentally inventoried the possibilities. It was hardly a new exercise. In recent years my son's life had become a litany of criminal behavior: drug abuse, thefts, arrests, prison time. And, while one never gets accustomed to midnight calls from jail, the dealing with lawyers, or visitations to courtrooms, there comes a time when the numbing regularity of such events takes a toll. Each time the disappointment is just as real, just as painful. But the element of surprise gradually erodes to the expected.

"What's he done?" I stopped short of adding an angry, sarcastic "this time."

Pat began shaking her head, moving her hands to her face in an attempt to hide the tears that had again begun to flow. "He's killed Annette," she said in a pained whisper I could barely hear.

Standing in the doorway, I felt for a moment that my legs would not support me. A cold, numbing ache ran through my body, stealing away every drop of energy. I became vaguely aware that my hands were shaking uncontrollably and hid them away, plunging them deep into the pockets of my jacket.

How desperately I wanted my wife to be mistaken. I wanted to wake suddenly and learn that the scene had been scripted from nothing more than a horrible dream. I could summon no logical thinking that would allow acceptance of what she'd said despite the fact it had been relayed by a person I trusted above all others. I wanted to hide away, to run from this evil monster that had so abruptly invaded my world.

In truth, I had long been resigned to the disturbing fact that my son, at the time twenty-five years old, had chosen a life's path of self-destructive behavior. No amount of pleading or prayer, visits to clinics and psychologists' offices, had altered his course. With each parole from prison, I had desperately hoped for some sudden miracle of change while, at the same time, privately counting the days until he would be found guilty of a new, senseless crime and returned to a cell in some faraway place.

But murder, man's ultimate inhumanity to man, committed by my own flesh and blood? It was impossible.

The only detail that Pat had been given was that Anson had been arrested at the Dallas apartment of his ex-wife earlier in the day and was being held in the county jail.

"What are you going to do?" she asked.

"I guess I'd better make some calls."

For some time I sat alone in my office, staring across the desk at the phone, dreading the conversation that awaited. The pleasant afternoon and images of smiling young faces had been erased by the knowledge that as I had read from a happy fairy tale on one side of town a disquieting nightmare was being played out on the other.

THE VOICE OF Detective T. J. Barnes was not what television scriptwriters have trained us to expect from those working out of police station Homicide Divisions. Instead of gruff and world-weary, it was pleasant and professional. And, for some reason, sounded younger that I had expected.

There was a brief but noticeable silence on his end of the line after I identified myself and explained that I had just learned that my son had been taken into custody.

"I would," I said, "appreciate anything you can tell me about what's happened."

His voice quickly took on a dispassionate, businesslike tone. "Sir, Anson Eugene Stowers was arrested today at the Timberline Apartments and charged with the murder of his wife . . . I'm sorry, his ex-wife . . . Annette Robinson Stowers, age twenty-five, and is now being held in the Lew Sterrett jail." I sensed that he was leafing through a case file as he spoke.

"According to what he told us, he killed her yesterday . . . sometime around one in the afternoon. We received an anonymous call earlier today from a resident of the apartment complex who Anson had tried to sell some of the deceased's jewelry to. Our informant said that he had reason to believe a murder had been committed."

When the police had knocked on the door of Apartment 218, the detective explained, Anson answered and made no attempt to keep them from coming inside. At the foot of the bed in an adjoining room, investigators found the body, wrapped in bedsheets and a rug.

"He told us," Detective Barnes said, "that she had wanted him to kill her."

I didn't want to hear any more, yet if I was to make any sense of the sinister tragedy, I had to know. Only after I specifically asked did the officer inform me that Annette had been bludgeoned, strangled, and stabbed.

Anson, he said, had already given a confession.

"Did he say anything else?"

"When we entered the apartment," the detective replied, "he told us that if he'd had just twelve more hours we would never have found him or the body."

How often, I wondered, had the officer been through similar conversations? How many apartments had he walked into during his career to view bloody scenes that would become the next day's headlines? Did it ever get easy? And how did he manage to put it all behind him when his shift ended?

I'm not sure how long I sat there after hanging up, pondering the surrealistic sequence of events. It was that time of year when evenings had begun arriving early, and only when Pat quietly entered and turned on a lamp did I realize that darkness had fallen.

"Are you okay?" she asked as she placed an arm over my shoulder.

"I will be."

Fortunately, she did not question the manner in which I planned to accomplish such a task.

In time the phone began to ring. Pat took the calls, most of them from reporters asking for confirmation that Anson was, in fact, my son and for some statement from me. What could I possibly say?

For years I had worked as a reporter and had, on occasion, been required to perform the same difficult, intrusive task. It was, very simply, part of the job, and I knew no journalist who enjoyed it.

Some years earlier, while still working for the *Dallas Morning News*, I had been dispatched to a small town in East Texas to do a story on a gifted sixteen-year-old amateur boxer who had died in a plane crash while returning home from an international tournament in Europe. My assignment had been to talk with the townspeople and get their reaction to the tragedy.

I had spent most of the day talking with fellow students, the youngster's teachers, his coach, leaving the most difficult interview for last. Finally, I had knocked on the door of the boy's home and identified myself to his mother. A large, sad-faced woman dressed in a terry cloth robe graciously welcomed me into her modest house. On a mantel in the small, well-kept living room were lined a number of carefully polished trophies won by her son.

I was surprised to find her alone, without friends or relatives to care for her in her time of grief. With little prompting she talked pridefully, lovingly of her son. A good boy. A good student. Never in any trouble. His daddy had died in a work-related accident when his son was just a baby. Her boy, she observed, was too kind, really, to have attained the degree of success he had in such a violent sport. "But," she said, "he was always telling me he was going to be a professional one day and make a lot of money so he could buy me a new house."

In the course of my half-hour visit she had not cried. Only the haunting, melancholic sound of her voice suggested the terrible pain she was suffering. As I rose to leave, she stood before me and forced a heartbreaking smile. "Thank you for coming and letting me talk about my boy."

Responding to a sudden urge, I reached out and hugged her. And in that spontaneous moment, shared between total strangers, her grief exploded. Holding tightly to me, her entire body shook as she alternately sobbed and screamed angry curses at her fate.

Indeed, the journalist's job is not always easy.

It was something I tried to bear in mind as the story of my son's crime led off the ten o'clock television news. The anchor who read the story seemed not nearly as concerned about the murder or the victim as he was about the fact that it involved "the son of a well-known local author who, ironically, has written extensively about crime."

As he spoke, dust jackets of several of my books appeared on the screen.

I did not attend Annette's funeral. For several days I agonized over whether or not to call her parents before it occurred to me that I did not even know their names. Even before she and Anson had married, I had been under the impression that Annette lived not at home but with her grandmother, and it never occurred to me to pry about her relationship with her mother and father.

Had I called them, what would I have said? In their eyes, no doubt, I was their hated enemy just as surely as was my son. They had suffered an overwhelming, unfathomable loss, and doubtless their anger had spread quickly to me. I had fathered the person who took their daughter's life, and while not a sin for which I could be prosecuted, it was reason enough for their blame.

I'd seen the hard-drawn line, separating the families of the victim and the relatives of the defendant, at every trial I'd ever attended.

FOR DAYS AFTER THE NEWS of Annette's death, I wandered through a thick, enabling fog. Pat, along with a number of supportive friends, repeatedly assured me that I should not feel blame for the unthinkable tragedy. In truth, I didn't. Instead, the emotion I found myself battling was one of overwhelming sadness, born of a resignation that all past efforts, however frail and faulted, to help my son toward a healthy, productive life had gone for naught.

He had finally ventured far beyond the reach of any saving lifeline I could throw.

How, I wondered, could this have happened? What evil compass had pointed the way toward such tragedy?

TWO

ABILENE, Texas, in the early sixties was light-years removed from the peace-and-love lifestyle that was blooming wildly throughout much of the nation. A city of 90,000, it was the shining, self-rightous buckle of the West Texas Bible Belt, boasting three denominational colleges and more churches per capita than any community of similar size in the country. The cotton and oil industries provided the foundation of its economy, but ironclad Christian values and good neighbor patriotism were its real stock and trade. That and its high school athletic teams, which collected state championships with envied regularity.

Early in the summer of 1962 while home from my sophomore year at the University of Texas, I had begun dating a pretty, brown-eyed high school senior-to-be named Jana Freeman. We saw movies together at the downtown Paramount Theater, enjoyed late-evening pizzas at the first restaurant in Abilene to offer such exotic fare, and joined friends for Cokes and fries at the local curb service hangout. It was *American Grafitti*-in-the-boonies; all in all a happy, carefree time that showed no hint of ending.

Then, just weeks before I was to return to college, Jana tearfully confided to me that she was pregnant.

For days that followed I reported to my summer job with the Texas State Highway Department without benefit of sleep, an overwhelming panic accompanying me like some black, menacing storm cloud. I was going to be a father, and the thought was the most fearful thing I'd ever experienced.

It was a time when teenage pregnancy was neither commonplace nor socially accepted, especially in a small West Texas town where half the population was given to quoting scripture at the sight of a beer can. It carried with it a devastating stigma, particularly for a teenage girl, that was certain to give rise to cruel whispers and feelings of rampant guilt. It was something that simply did not happen in "nice" families, to "good" kids.

One evening, as we sat alone at a picnic table in the darkened city park, discussing the problem that had become the sudden focus of both our lives, I asked her to marry me.

I had saved some money during the summer, I explained, and

my athletic scholarship at the University of Texas would cover the cost of off-campus housing. And the sports editor of the Austin American-Statesman had promised me a part-time job once school resumed. If she was willing to give it a try, I told her, I felt we could make it. I promised to do my best to take care of her.

It was, I knew, a proposal that ignored a multitude of problems. How could people just nineteen and seventeen years old be certain of their feelings for each other? Was the prospect of a child enough to bond a relationship, fueling its growth into something durable and long-standing? And what of the youthful experiences that would be lost to her, the well-earned joys of her final year of high school, the separation from family and friends?

The gravity of the situation, however, did not offer the luxury of dwelling on such issues.

"I think," she said, "that I would like being your wife and living in Austin."

And so it was that I returned to college a married man, a father-to-be, both frightened and excited about what the future had in store.

DESPITE MY ENCOURAGEMENT, Jana opted not to enroll in one of the Austin high schools. Instead, she busied her days decorating our small upstairs apartment, which was located just a few blocks from the campus. In the evenings she helped me with my studies and occasionally prepared meals for fellow members of the track team who dropped in with bulging grocery bags. We went to campus movies, where admission was only a dime, attended weekend football games, and took long drives into the picturesque rolling countryside. We raised an orphaned squirrel that I often carried in my jacket pocket on walks to and from the campus.

Being married and expecting a child grew on me quickly. Though moments of concern continued to pay uneasy visits, they always gave way to the discovery of a new meaning and responsibility to my life as I found myself eagerly looking forward to the arrival of the baby.

Our biggest problem was one shared by most newlyweds: money. Determined not to seek financial assistance from our parents, we lived on a budget so thin it was almost transparent. For my work on the *Daily Texan,* the campus newspaper, I received a small monthly stipend. Two nights a week I answered phones and wrote accounts of high school football games at the *Austin American-Statesman.* On Saturdays I sold souvenir programs prior to the football games.

If there was a way to make a buck, I embraced it. In the evenings, when my work for the *Daily Texan* was done, I slipped a folded grocery bag from my desk and began a trek across campus. By the time I arrived home the sack would be filled with discarded soft drink bottles, each worth a two-cent refund, which I stored in the bottom of our closet in anticipation of cash needed for an emergency.

And while things financial were a constant concern, sleep became my worst adversary. Days simply didn't offer enough time to attend to all the responsibilities I was attempting to juggle.

Only after a summons to the office of the dean of men at the beginning of the second semester was I forced to take weary stock of what was occurring in my life. Concerned that my already fragile grades had slipped, he peered at my records through reading glasses perched precariously on the bridge of his nose.

"I understand, Mr. Stowers, that you are enrolled for eighteen hours this semester," he said.

"Yes, sir."

"And that you are a member of our track team, required to train daily and attend meets each weekend in the spring."

"Yes, sir."

"And you're writing regularly for the *Daily Texan*."

"That's right."

"You also work part-time at the Austin paper."

I was amazed at how much he knew of my activities. "Yes, sir."

"Have I missed anything?"

"My wife and I are expecting a child."

He slowly shook his head and leaned back in the oversize leather chair, removing his glasses and placing them atop the manila folder, which contained my none-too-impresive records. For several seconds he was silent, as if lost in thought. "Young man," he finally said, "it is my suggestion that you take a hard look at your activities and determine as quickly as possible where you might cut back."

I stopped short of asking where he thought such reduction should take place. My athletic scholarship had allowed me to enroll in college in the first place. And without the income from the part-time jobs, doctor bills would go unpaid and groceries would be hard to come by. If I reduced the number of courses I was taking, graduation wasn't likely to occur until sometime in the next century.

Still, he had made a valid point, one I pondered throughout the remainder of the day.

In truth, it had not been the prospect of higher education that had lured me to Austin in the first place. I had gone there to continue my athletic career; satisfactory academic performance was nothing more than a necessary evil to maintain my eligibility. I was, quite honestly, a jock's jock. Certainly no high school teacher or university professor had ever pointed to me as an exemplary student.

Still, the time had finally come when I had to accept the fact that my future as a sprinter promised no legitimate shot at Olympic glory. Though I had managed to earn my letter as a relay member, I was hardly a star participant on the team. A shift in priorities had begun to take place.

Despite my lukewarm attitude toward the academic life, the university had provided me an introduction to a profession I was dead set on pursuing. Becoming a newspaperman, a writer, had grown quickly into a passion. Even with the limited exposure I'd had, I'd fallen in love with journalism's hectic pace, deadlines, and the priceless satisfaction of seeing my byline atop a story.

I knew what I wanted to do with my life, was impatient to get on with it, and thus placed a long-distance call to the editor of my hometown paper, asking if he had any openings in his sports department. I was delighted to learn that a job was available.

It paid seventy-five dollars per week, I excitedly told Jana.

Within days I had left college life and athletic pursuits behind and, just shy of my twentieth birthday, became a full-time newspaperman.

And had gathered my last pop bottle.

ON A SUNDAY EVENING in May of 1963 I was at work in the sports department, sorting and editing stories for the next day's edition, when a neighbor phoned to say Jana had gone into labor and that he and his wife were driving her to the hospital. Suddenly ball scores, golf tournament results, and how the Yankees' Roger Maris was doing in his bid to rewrite home run history became quickly forgotten trivia as I hurried from the building.

The wait was remarkably brief. Without the slightest complication, Jana delivered a healthy baby boy just after midnight. Shortly thereafter I was introduced to my son, looking into eyes so like his mother's that blinked up at me in utter bewilderment. I held him close, feeling his sweet breath against my cheek, touched his smooth olive skin, soft as rose petals, and inspected tiny, wrinkled fingers, all the while swept away by the mind boggling wonder of creation.

BECOMING A PARENT, particularly when only briefly removed from childhood yourself, ranks as one of life's most nerve-racking experiences. The sudden responsibility of caring for an infant helpless even to explain the cause for its midnight tears or to demand remedies that will scare away fevers and cholic and the pains of teething borders on the overwhelming. To inexperienced and unprepared parents, babies are initially viewed as more fragile than the finest of china, giving rise to an ever present wariness and worry no child-rearing how-to book can explain. Yet there is some cosmic order, defying all scientific explanation, which finally allows mom and dad to quit tiptoeing to the crib hourly to check on breathing and instead steal precious rest until time for the next feeding.

In time we learned that a late-night car ride would often induce sleep far better than a rocking chair, and that the undetected presence of the family cat in the playpen did not mean—as the old wives' tale would have had us believe—that he was there on an evil mission to suck the life's breath from our unsuspecting newborn.

Which is to say we also matured, growing, quite literally, with our child until gradually able to relax and enjoy the idea of having a new member of the family. In time, the anxiety of parenthood became salved by the warmth and simple pleasure of watching our son grow.

From the day of his arrival home from the hospital, Anson was a strong, healthy child, nurtured and tended to by a loving mother who had adapted quickly to her task. It seemed the best of times. We were a family ready to set out on an exciting adventure certain to be filled with new discoveries we'd not yet even imagined.

That dark days might lie ahead was a possibility that did not warrant even the slightest consideration.

SOCIETY HAS LONG SENT out mixed signals about the male's role in the family structure. Library shelves are filled to bursting with a confusing maze of psychobabble that outlines the duties of husband and helpmate, father and friend, provider and protector. Some insist that the early nurturing of a child falls more to the mother; others angrily lash out at absentee dads too absorbed in careers to take their turn at changing diapers, warming a bottle, or being on time for the monthly PTA meetings.

In the years that followed Anson's birth, I attempted to walk the fine line between family and career. Daily journalism bears little resemblance to the nine-to-five responsibilities of loan officers and shop clerks. Its hours are long and varied, often requiring spur-of-the-moment travel. More weekends than I can recall were spent away from home. I was solely to blame for countless dinners that grew cold and last-minute changes of plans made necessary by some breaking story it was my job to report.

And there were the moves. The early stages of one's newspaper career are, by some ancient decree, a nomadic undertaking. If a reporter is determined to advance in his profession, both financially and to larger, more prestigious positions, job changes are all but mandatory. Thus, in Anson's early childhood days we changed addresses with great regularity. The lure of a fifty-dollar-per-week pay increase sent us traveling west from Abilene to Roswell, New Mexico. Three years later we were back in Texas, where the *Lubbock Avalanche-Journal* became my professional home. Anson was almost five when, late in 1967, we left there en route to Dallas.

While I worked as a sportswriter for the *Dallas Morning News* our second son, Ashley, was born. And though the excitement and anticipation of his arrival were no less than we had experienced with Anson, the apprehension was greatly diminished. The old adage that the arrival of the first child is a fearful experience while the second is to be enjoyed, we would learn, held great credence. Redheaded and bright-eyed, Ashley arrived on the eleventh day of the new year, and no one was more pleased than his older brother. Anson, in his five-year-old wisdom, had for months assured us that he would be welcoming home a baby brother, and the news that his forecast had come true pleased him greatly. The morning following the delivery I took him to the hospital to meet his new brother.

Ashley was cradled in Jana's arms as we entered the room, and

I watched as Anson tiptoed to the side of the bed, a look of wonder illuminating his face. He leaned over to peek beneath the downy blanket at the tiny figure whose eyes blinked up at him quizzically, as if in an effort to determine who this giant stranger might be.

"This is your new brother," Jana said.

Anson smiled and said nothing for a moment, completely mesmerized, then tentatively extended a finger to a miniature hand that reached up toward him.

"Can I kiss him?" Anson asked.

As he knelt forward, gently placing his lips on the forehead of his brother, I wished more than at any other time in my life I'd had a camera to forever freeze the moment.

If Anson felt any jealousy toward the sudden shift of attention to the needs of his infant brother, it was not visable. Rather, he eagerly stood ready to help with feedings and oversee baths, and would stand by the crib for long stretches of time, monitoring his brother's sleep and awaiting the time he would wake, ready to play.

Ashley's presence, then, provided Anson with a new and exciting feeling of importance; the role of "big brother" offered him his first encounter with purpose and responsibility.

It is an attitude he would hold strongly to, even in trying times to come. Despite all his eventual problems and missteps, Anson would remain always protective of his younger brother. And as Ashley grew, taking his first steps, speaking his first words, it was obvious that he felt a special delight in the loving attention of his big brother.

It was, I felt, as things should be.

WHILE THE INTERMITTENT TRAVELS would continue through the first ten years of my professional life, the moves were made without complaint from Jana or any noticeable damage to the psyches of our children.

Along the way, I attended Cub Scout meetings, coached Anson's peewee softball team, lent help with science fair projects, and always managed to get back from whatever trip I'd been sent on in time to attend the annual family day at Six Flags, a day set aside by management of the amusement park for newspeople and their children. If I missed a birthday or holiday or school play, I honestly don't recall it. Which is to say that in retrospect I'm unable to judge the family situation in which our children were raised as abnormal. My wife stayed at home, attending their daily needs; I went off to work each day, just as millions of other fathers did.

And if there were signs that Anson was somehow troubled during the early stages of his life, they went undetected. Memory offers, in fact, but one occurrence that was at the time cause for concern.

One afternoon, his second-grade teacher phoned and requested that we come to school for a conference. Anson, she would later explain, had stolen a small gold chain and locket belonging to one of the girls in his class. Later in the day he had wrapped the locket in tissue and, during recess, proudly presented it to the teacher as a gift. Despite undeniable proof that the trinket was, in fact, the same one the girl had reported missing, Anson had adamantly denied the theft.

It being my first parental encounter with such behavior, I pondered appropriate punishment not only for stealing but also for what I deemed the greater crime of refusing to tell the truth. Only after repeated questioning of why he had taken the locket did he finally admit his childish reason: He liked his teacher very much and simply wanted to give her a present.

The next day, after school had ended, I drove him to a local flower shop where I urged him to pick out a bouquet to give to his teacher. I then returned him to the school and accompanied him as he entered to find her still in her classroom, grading papers. Bashfully, he presented her the flowers and apologized for the previous day's behavior. Our next stop was the home of the girl whose locket had been taken. There, his punishment ended with another bashful apology.

And the "crisis," hardly different from that faced by many children and parents at some time, passed.

Still, in the years to come, I would find myself looking back on those days, searching for signs I'd overlooked, occurrences that might have raised some red flag I was too blind or busy to notice. In recent days, in fact, I've spent a great deal of time drawing mental comparisons between my childhood and Anson's, searching for some reason why a father and son could be so different.

As a youngster I had followed my parents from one dry-bed West Texas town to another while my father pursued his career as a depot agent for the Santa Fe railroad. We rarely spent more than a year in the same town. As a ninth grader, in fact, I recall attending three schools in as many towns, playing football at one, basketball at another, and running on the track team at still another.

With each move I had felt the normal youthful sadness at leaving friends and familiar places behind, but the melancholy was generally short-lived. There were always new friends to be made, new sports teams to try out for.

But if my family's wanderings left psychological scars, I am unaware of them. Whatever sadness I felt at leaving one place was always overshadowed by the new sense of excitement and adventure that accompanied the prospect of moving to another. The familiar comfort of roots and stability is universally cherished, and I suppose I would have been perfectly happy to have grown up in the same house on the same block in the same town. But it was never an option made available, nor was it something I recall longing for consciously. My parents were chasing some brass ring I knew nothing about, and it was simply my lot in life to follow along.

In my youth I had been obsessed with sports and enjoyed modest success at whatever game was in season. It became my easy entrée into a new fraternity, the basis for quickly made friendships. If we moved in the summer, I immediately sought a Little League baseball team to join. If it was fall, football awaited. The winter offered basketball, and in the spring a track team always needed another runner.

Overly nostalgic recollections aside, the rural outposts of my youth offered a quieter, simpler lifestyle. While two-dollar woes and second-lien finances were a constant source of concerned conversation between my parents, I have no recollection of ever being made to feel socially inferior by friends who lived in better homes or whose mom and dad drove newer cars. The trappings of wealth, in fact, seemed unimportant and were generally ignored by those of my generation. I remember little peer pressure like that which exists in today's young society, and the closest I ever came to involvement with drugs was the night a group of us slipped into a local drive-in to view a forbidden feature titled *Mary Jane—Killer Weed*. The plot of the grainy black-and-white film escapes me except for the fact that a young actress turned immediately into sex-starved trash after one innocent experiment with marijuana.

In the time of my youth, adults argued over life's hardships, sometimes with great vigor, but managed to resolve their differences long before lawyers were ever called. I'm hard pressed to remember an acquaintance whose parents had split up. The family status quo, then, was rarely questioned.

My parents offered guidance and support but little pressure. If they harbored undue concern for my future, I was unaware of it. Life then was lived on a day-by-day, whatever-will-be basis. Only through the generosity of an athletic scholarship was I eventually able to become the first member of my family to darken a college door.

Which is to say I grew up happy, naive, and blissfully ignorant of the social ills plaguing the world. I was neither abused nor deprived and felt no parental pressures beyond the urging to do my homework, join the family in church on Sunday mornings, and stay out of trouble. To have rebelled against such adult demands was unthinkable.

I simply took it for granted that my parents were and would forever be an inseparable team.

How different it would be for my own children.

THE TIME WOULD EVENTUALLY COME when the demands of my job began to wear on Jana. The signs at first were subtle, no doubt there for some time before I even recognized them. Too many late nights at the office and too much travel, I could only assume, had finally begun to take a toll. I sensed an unhappiness that I'd never before seen in my wife, and it troubled me greatly.

Efforts to discuss whatever problems existed, however, were to no avail. If there was cause for the new sadness in Jana's eyes, reason for the distance that had begun to develop between us, she was of no mind to share it.

Perhaps the greatest shortcoming of our marriage had been a mutual pattern of dismissing problems that occurred without ever really talking them out or determining their cause. In time, as difficulties became more frequent, it was easier simply to act as if nothing had happened, as if some miracle would do the mending while we blindly turned our heads and kept going. We rarely had conversations that cleared the air but instead just gave each other a shrug of resignation that left in its aftermath growing doubt and mistrust. We were not mature enough—or smart enough—to recognize the eroding process that was under way. Repeatedly, I willingly closed my eyes to the problems, hoping the darkness would make them disappear.

Money became an ever-growing cancer. Once, early in our marriage, Jana had complained to my father that, as he phrased it, I was "too tight with a dollar," that I refused to trust her with the slightest financial responsibility. Picking his words carefully, he had, for one of the first times I could remember, offered me marital advice. "Let her show you that she can manage the money," he said. "Hell, I haven't written a check for a bill since your mother and I got married." With that he placed his arm around my shoulder and smiled. "You know," he added, "the truth is you *are* a little on the tight side."

It was a painful fact to accept. But one founded in truth. The idea of being in debt, owing money I did not have, frightened me. Yet I took his advice and turned the family finances over to my wife with an apology for the lack of faith I'd displayed. And in short order our problems worsened. Soon, I began receiving calls at work, inquiring why the rent payment had not been made or bills had gone overlooked. Routinely, overdraft notifications arrived from the bank. And each time that I asked Jana for some explanation I got nothing but vague, defensive answers. She thought she had paid this bill; she didn't know that one was due; she didn't know where the money had gone.

It was just the beginning. In time our life became a constant stream of evasive answers, one spoken to cover another.

An officer at a bank where I had not had an account in years telephoned me to express concern over the fact I was seriously overdrawn. "Our annual audit is coming up," he said, "and we'd like to get this matter cleared up."

I was nonplussed, not only by the shot-to-the-gut realization I was in the deepest financial trouble of my life but also by the incredibly unprofessional practice of the bank. "As far as I know I don't even have an account there. How in the hell could you let *anyone* get that far overdrawn?"

"Your wife explained to us when she opened the account that the method of payment for the magazine articles and books you write is sporadic, that you receive sizable payments only when your work is completed. We assumed—"

"I don't know anything about this," I interrupted.

There was a silent pause. Then, in a tone that was almost apologetic, he said, "Frankly, I've been afraid of that for some time now."

Only when Jana's father, who did business at the same bank—

which was, I had to assume, the only reason she was allowed to open the account in the first place—spoke with the president and heard the same story I did was she finally forced to admit to her secret spending. She insisted that she had no idea what all the money had been spent on. It would, she tearfully promised, never happen again.

I heard no more from the bank and only later suspicioned that Jana's father, aware that I didn't have the finances to repay the debt, had somehow taken care of the matter. The incident became yet another of those about which I chose to bury my head.

And for a time things seemed to improve. With great relief, I began to believe our life would return to a sense of normalcy. Then, one evening, I arrived home earlier than expected to find several new, expensive dresses draped across a chair. Jana's explanation was that a friend had purchased them, then abruptly decided they were not to her liking once she got home with them.

"She gave them to me," Jana said.

"Couldn't she have returned them?" I asked. "The price tags are still on them."

Jana only shrugged.

It angered me that she felt I might believe such an improbable story. "Why the hell can't you just tell me the truth? Why are you lying to me?"

"I'm not," she deadpanned, then turned and left the room.

It was a routine that would be played out again and again. In time it became impossible to believe anything she told me. Frantic for some solution, I even suggested that she see a counselor who might help her resolve whatever problems she was dealing with. She found the idea amusing. "Maybe," she suggested, "*you're the one who needs help.*"

I wondered if, perhaps, she was right. I never had any *proof* that she lied about the spending.

Had she, I wondered, come to a point in life where she was privately mourning the loss of her own youth to the sudden responsibilities of marriage and motherhood? Had her daily routine become so consumed by caring for the children and the household that it left her with no life of her own? What had prompted the rash of untruths that had become so commonplace, the sudden free spending? Could it be that she viewed my dedication to my work as some evil mistress over which she had no control?

They were questions to which she volunteered no answers.

FOR SOME TIME I had been weighing my own future, and I was more and more determined that newspaper work would not be the alpha and omega of my career as a writer. I envied greatly those who had advanced to writing lengthy magazine pieces and admired those with talent enough to author books. For some time I had made an effort to gain a foothold on what I considered the next step up the professional ladder. Working nights, I had begun to write and submit articles to a variety of publications and hounded book publishers for the opportunity to prove I could produce.

When I was offered a modest contract to author a nonfiction book about following the state's premier high school football team through a season, I gained the courage to venture into the world of freelance writing.

I looked ahead to a new project and new lifestyle with

renewed enthusiasm, eagerly envisioning the day when I would see my name on the cover of a book. And, being able to work at home, I hoped, would resolve whatever problems threatened my marriage.

There would, I was soon to learn, be no resolution.

Three

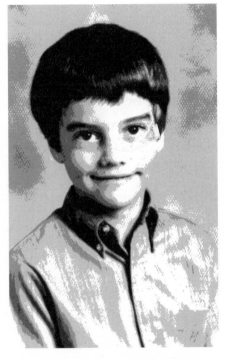

ON A SUMMER EVENING in 1973 I sat with the boys at a redwood picnic table in the backyard, searching for words to explain something I myself did not completely understand.

"I've moved into an apartment," I said, doing my best to put a casual twist on an event that I knew full well was going to dramatically alter our lives. I made no mention of the late-night discussions their mother and I had been having recently; said nothing of the fact she had urged the separation, insisting that she needed time alone so she might "think things out." I left unsaid my growing awareness that our eleven-year marriage was coming to an end. Jana had not mentioned divorce, but I was certain it was on her mind. Once I was out of the house, I knew, it would soon become a reality. I'd seen it happen to too many other couples.

What else was I to do? If I hadn't volunteered to leave, she would have done so, removing the children from a comfortable home and a familiar neighborhood. The only logical alternative had been for me to go.

"Why?" Anson asked, his big brown eyes searching. Ashley, his chin resting in the palms of his small hands, silently awaited my answer.

At that moment I desperately wished for wisdom I did not possess and for them to be older and more able to comprehend the obvious. But I could not find an honest, satisfactory answer for his simple question.

"Your mother and I have decided we just need a little time away from each other," I finally said. I tried to assure them nothing they had done was the cause for the decision. I told them that I loved them and would see them daily. In a manner of speaking, I was offering up the false promise that things would go on normally when, in fact, they were never again going to be the same.

It was near dark when Jana appeared at the back door to call the boys in for dinner. It was also my signal to leave, taking with me a secret I would hide from my children for years to come.

FOR MONTHS I HAD BATTLED with private suspicions that my wife was having an affair. In time, I even became relatively certain who she was seeing—a man I knew from around the neighborhood—but I made no real effort to prove my case. I simply did not want to believe it, felt an uneasy guilt at my unproven concern, and hoped that I was wrong. If there was truth to be learned, I didn't want to face it.

One evening, long after the children had gone to bed, Jana and I sat talking. The atmosphere in which we were living had begun to gnaw at me, begging for some resolution.

"I know you're very unhappy," I said, "but what I don't know is why. If there's something I can do, you have to make me aware of it."

Jana sat silently, her face a mask of sadness.

"Why are you so miserable?"

"I don't know."

Finally, I blurted out the question I'd dreaded asking. "Is there someone else?"

"No," she insisted. "I just need some time to myself."

"You want me to move out?"

Tears moistened her eyes as she looked across the room at me for several silent seconds. Slowly, she nodded her head. Her answer was yes, and with it came the cold, real awareness that we had somehow arrived at a point of no return.

The following day I had gone in search of a furnished apartment.

I didn't want my marriage to end. The blame for whatever problems existed, I decided, rested squarely on my shoulders. I had traveled too much, criticized too often, focused too single-mindedly on my work. If Jana had felt need for the companionship of someone else, the blame was mine and mine alone. The more I contemplated the situation, the longer my list of personal shortcomings grew.

And in the midst of this self-flagellation, I chose to ignore the other side of the coin. I willingly granted blanket forgiveness. I could, I was convinced, even forgive infidelity.

Such were the irrational, misguided thoughts that occupied my every waking moment in the aftermath of our separation. There was no moment of clear thinking, only the desperate focus on attempting to mend something unmendable. She was my wife, the mother of my children, and I wanted things to be right again.

In the cell-like confines of my rented apartment, I did no work. Instead I wallowed in self-pity. I tried to read, but the pages might just as well have been blank. I cooked meals that went uneaten and slept very little. I was stranded in a limbo unlike anything I'd ever known, overwhelmed by a state of depression that ultimately caused me to begin wondering about my mental well-being. If I was not going crazy, it was as close as I ever wanted to come.

My only touch with reality came when I spent time with the boys. Though puzzled by the new living arrangement, they asked no questions during their visits, and I made no attempt at further explanation. They seemed fine, and I found myself envying their remarkable gift of adaptability and youthful innocence.

It took the arrival of the petition for divorce to jar me back to my senses. As I read through the legal jargon that sounded the end of my marriage, anger began to nibble away at the edges of the pain. I wished she had been honest enough to admit she was planning on filing for divorce, eliminating the cruel charade of needing time alone to think things through. Why hadn't she simply said she was in love with someone else? What gave her the right to destroy my life?

While I entertained no thoughts of contesting the divorce, I did visit several attorneys to discuss something I'd given a great deal of thought to since the separation. I wanted custody of my sons. I was confident that I could raise them properly, that we could continue to be a family even in the absence of their mother.

It was an idea whose time had not yet come. The response of each lawyer with whom I spoke was the same: Chances of a Texas judge granting conservatorship to a father simply did not exist.

One attorney went so far as to describe the last custody case he'd handled at the request of an anguished dad. "I proved that the kids' mother was a prostitute, the sorriest, sleaziest bitch you've ever imagined. She was a certified junkie and treated her children badly, leaving them home alone while she went out and turned tricks and got her next fix. Then she would sleep all day, leaving the kids to fend for themselves.

"The father, meanwhile, was a decent guy. He was a hard worker, loved his children more than anything in the world, and was ready to do everything in his power to provide them a quality life.

"And you know what? It took about ten seconds for the judge to rule that those poor children should stay with their sorry-ass mother. The whole thing made me sick.

"What I'm telling you, as honestly as I know how, is that you would be wasting your time and money trying to get custody. The best you're going to get is a visitation schedule you can live with."

With only slight variation, I heard the same advice from everyone.

In time, my feelings of anger, self-doubt, and disappointment evolved into an aimless attempt to determine the course of my own life. No miracle, I slowly began to realize, was going to restore our marriage. Still, the ache that accompanied seeing Jana almost daily when I picked up the boys or she dropped them by was as real as any physical pain I'd ever known. On the one hand, I was convinced that I still loved her. At the same time, my resentment toward her grew as she continued steadfastly to deny her involvement with another man. Only after I angrily suggested that I might embarass her lover publicly, alerting others to the affair, did she finally admit the relationship, frantically pleading with me not to involve his family.

That she expressed more concern for their emotional welfare than mine or her own children's served as a dramatic wake-up call.

The television sitcom suggestion of amicable divorce ending in handshakes and pledges of lifelong friendships, I quickly realized, was nothing more than grade-A, pasteurized bullshit—a fantasy that came along about as often as Halley's Comet.

What I had to determine was how to jump-start my own life. To do so, I had to get away, put distance between myself and daily reminders of the disruption of my world. Even the most casual encounter with my soon-to-be-ex wife was agonizing. Passing her secret lover on the street caused a boil of anger that was barely controllable. I considered confronting him, even going to his wife and telling her that she too would soon have to deal with the cruelties I was experiencing, that her young children would be robbed of the safety and comfort of a family unit.

I was becoming mean-spirited, filled with ugly thoughts that, in more lucid moments, were frightening. I had to get away. But to where?

THERE IS NO WAY to describe properly the inner feeling of well-being that comes from having a sense of place.

Whether home is an address in an upscale Beverly Hills neighborhood or a rundown tenement in the Bronx, it is a person's single most stabilizing factor. You may snobbishly praise its luxury and location or scream curses at its faulty plumbing and meddling neighbors, but deep inside there is always the knowledge that it is your small spot in the universe. It is where you are to be, your soul's resting place, the home to which you will always return for shelter from the complexities of the outside world.

It fell to me to find a new place to be. And I had no idea in which direction to search. Giving a fumbling explanation to Anson and Ashley that I would soon be leaving town, assuring them that no matter how far I traveled we would see each other regularly, I took my overdue leave.

Had I been in a more pleasant frame of mind, my quest for a new home, a new beginning, might have been an adventure. I drove to New York to pay an unannounced visit to the surprised editor of a soon-to-be-published book I'd written. I visited my younger sister, Laurie, in Dallas. I spent most of a week on the couch of a friend in Austin, attending a University of Texas football game and a concert by country-and-western balladeer Tom T. Hall. Late one night I arrived in Houston, having not the slightest idea why I had traveled there. I drove aimlessly along the backroads of my West Texas homeland, spending nights in long-since-forgotten motels. I was killing time in small increments, mile by mile, minute by minute, day by day.

Throughout my solitary travels I tried vainly to convince myself that a sudden new freedom had been granted me. But, in truth, I wanted no part of it. The images of what I'd left behind rode along with me, haunting every mile. Never had I felt so alone. Or so cowardly, running from my own disappointments while leaving my sons behind.

I finally settled temporarily in Dallas and took a job on the loading docks of a truck freight line. With no creative juices flowing, the idea of sitting alone at a typewriter did not interest me in the least. A few months of hard, manual labor in the company of strangers, I decided, might speed along whatever transition I was going to have to make.

In retrospect, it may have been the most visible hint of mental instability I demonstrated. Working alongside brawny young men who looked as if they should be preparing for heavyweight-title bouts or college football season instead of loading household appliances and boxes of foodstuffs into the trailers of trucks, I struggled to carry my own load. The work was muscle-aching hard, the hours long. I concluded each shift with absolutely no feeling of accomplishment aside from sheer survival. In time, a subtle yet valuable lesson emerged: Any writer who laments the struggles and demands of his profession need only haul his wide-load butt down to the nearest freight loading dock for a few twelve-hour shifts of wrestling TVs and refrigerators, and then compare.

Which is to say it didn't take long for me to turn my thoughts back to the needs of New York book and magazine editors and renew my search for a new, permanant address.

At the invitation of a novelist friend named Giles Tippett, I drove south one weekend into the picturesque Texas Hill Country. Giles had selected a hillside house on the outskirts of Kerrville from which to write, having left the pollution, congestion, and soaring crime statistics of suburban Houston behind a couple of years earlier.

The lush landscape, the spring-fed streams, and the roadside fields of bluebonnets in bloom triggered a rush of forgotten memories of a wonderful summer spent nearby during my college days. At the encouragement of an old junior high coach, I had applied for work as a counselor at a boys' camp. For three glorious months I had supervised a cabin of ten-year-olds, teaching them how to swim, shoot a bow and arrow, pilot a canoe, ride horses, and find their way along nature trails that wound through the lush wilderness of the Camp LaJunta property.

For one reared in the dry-bed flatlands of West Texas, it had been a visit to a new, picture postcard world. Deer grazed along the roadsides and daintily sipped the cool waters of the gently flowing streams, gray squirrels played endless games of chase through the trees, and the wildflowers provided a flaming rainbow of colors.

It was not just the sights and sounds of the region that had made an impression on an eighteen-year-old briefly freed from the pressures of higher learning. Those who called the region home were friendly, their lifestyle simple and slow paced, attuned to the beauty and comfortable isolation of their surroundings.

Such were the thoughts that came rushing back on that spur-of-the-moment visit to an old friend. Here, it occurred to me, might be a good place to start over.

Thus, on a warm, sunny Saturday afternoon I took a drive through the cypress-dotted countryside, ultimately finding my way to a small community with the fascinating name of Comfort. Though I'd never been to—or, for that matter, even heard of—

the place before, I found its Old World atmosphere charming. In the downtown area, a hundred-year-old grocery still welcomed customers. The nearby drugstore offered a soda fountain that brought a flood of memories from a long-ago childhood. On the town square there was a library, and despite a population of only 1,500, a grand old movie theater continued to operate on weekends.

On the outskirts of town, youngsters on horseback stopped to water their mounts in the shallow, rock-bottomed Guadalupe River. I drove past the Little League playing field, stopped for a hamburger and beer in an old Santa Fe railroad depot that had been converted into a restaurant, and walked the awning-draped sidewalks of the small business district, past the meat market, dry cleaners, bank, post office, and the office of the weekly *Comfort News*.

By sheer accident or act of fate, I had stumbled onto a new starting place.

At the newspaper office I found the editor at work on the next week's edition and placed a classified ad: *Single Dallas writer, anxious to move to the Hill Country, seeks rental property in or around Comfort.* I left my name and my sister's telephone number, then drove back to Dallas to wait anxiously.

A week later I was en route to pick up the boys so they might accompany me as I returned to the Hill Country to look at the place I'd already decided I would soon call home.

A man named J. A. Langridge had telephoned from San Antonio, explaining that he owned 350 acres outside Comfort. In addition to the weekend house he and his wife regularly visited, he said, there was a fully furnished two-bedroom native stone hunting cabin, which he had remodeled and was interested in renting at a price that was within my budget. Additionally, he would expect the renter to keep an eye on the main house, alerting him to any problems that might arise in his absence.

When I explained that I hoped to be joined during the summer vacation months by my two young sons he voiced no concern. "There's not a better place in the world to raise kids," he said. "They'll love it."

FOR THE FIRST FEW MONTHS of my bucolic residency I relished the isolation, rising early to chase away the deer that ventured close enough to the house to play havoc with the small vegetable garden I'd planted, spending the mornings and early afternoons at my typewriter. Late in the day I hiked the nearby hills, followed the winding course of the creek, and fished the ponds my landlord had stocked with largemouth bass and a hybrid perch that gave battle only skilled fishermen dream of.

I ventured from my new home only when the pantry needed replenishing, an editor's assignment demanded travel, or to spend a day with the boys.

Pangs of loneliness sometimes visited, usually in the evenings as the sun disappeared beneath the tops of the cypress and cedars or as I sat outside at night, marveling at the vast canopy of stars visible without city lights to block them from view. In time the peaceful quiet, interrupted only by nature's gentle sounds, would override all feelings of melancholy. I liked where I was and counted the days until summer when Anson and Ashley could share these rural wonders with me.

Whether real or the product of a romantic imagination, I had located in a place better than I could ever have imagined.

EARLY ON A FEBRUARY MORNING in 1974 I received an unexpected call from Jana. Her voice was brittle and businesslike, more that of a stranger than of a person I'd intimately known for so many years.

"The boys want to come live with you," she said.

I waited in stunned silence for several seconds, anticipating some explanation. But there was none.

"When?"

"Right now," Jana replied. "I have their things ready."

I quickly drove into town, rented a U-Haul trailer, and was in Brownwood by midafternoon, surprised to find that everything belonging to the boys waited in the open garage—furniture, their toys and books, bicycles, and clothing stuffed into plastic garbage bags.

Fearing that there might be some last-minute change of heart, I didn't even bother to announce my arrival. Instead, I hurriedly began to load the trailer, sure that the noise I was making would soon alert Anson and Ashley to my presence.

In short order they raced out the door, smiling and apparently happy, and eagerly began to help with the loading. If there was any great trauma or sadness attached to their leave-taking, I did not detect it. Rather, I saw two youngsters looking ahead to a new adventure, and I felt the sudden warmth of a long-absent excitement.

Still, it was all very perplexing, and my mind filled with questions I dared not ask. Had Jana suddenly arrived at some generous decision that our children would actually be better off living with me, or had they simply become an unwanted burden to her new freedom? In truth, the reasons behind the decision mattered little. Jana offered no enlightenment when she finally appeared to hand me an envelope containing the boys' school records. She bent down and hugged each of them, promised to see them soon, and silently returned to the house.

Surely, I thought as we drove away, she must be feeling some measure of sadness at the fact her children were leaving. If so, she hid it well.

Before nightfall we were in Comfort, arranging their new room while talking of exciting days that lay ahead. Only when I mentioned enrolling them in school did I sense the first note of reservation.

I explained that I had passed the elementary school on numerous occasions; it looked like a really nice place. New friends, I tried to assure them, awaited.

It was Anson who finally admitted the concern he and his brother shared: "Tomorrow," he explained, "is Valentine's Day and we don't know anybody." How, he wondered, could they be expected to participate in the traditional exchange of cards during the class party that was certain to be held at the end of the day?

Such are the innocent crises faced by kindergarteners and third-graders.

The solution to the problem was to drive into town and purchase several packages of heart-shaped greeting cards. Each signed his name to what I guessed would be an ample number for the students who would be in their respective classes. Inasmuch as they lacked names for addressing each card, my suggestion was that they give their cards to the teacher and ask that she distribute them.

"But," I warned, "since no one knows you'll be enrolling in school, don't be disappointed when you don't get any cards in return."

The following afternoon, as they emerged from their first day at Comfort Elementary, both were all smiles, each carrying a paper sack filled with valentines personally addressed to them. Their teachers, careful to see no one was left out of the holiday occasion, had seen to it that each student addressed cards to the new boys in their class.

From that day, brightened for each by their educators' thoughtfulness, I knew Anson and Ashley were going to like their new home.

It is a remarkable human condition, I believe, that provides one the gift of magnifying the memories of good times while allowing the troubled moments to blur until they are all but forgotten. Now, years later, I remember those days in Comfort with great fondness. In my mind's eye the life we lived together there was as close to idyllic as one can realistically hope to achieve.

For Anson and Ashley, the Texas Hill Country was a rural wonderland awaiting endless exploration. In the spring they wandered through the dizzying colors of bluebonnets and indian paintbrush, followed by the newest member of the family, a feisty, lovable dachshund named Nemo. In summers the cool, clear creek that ran adjacent to the cabin served as a swimming hole by day, and the gentle sound of its nearby waterfall lent a peaceful sound to the night.

On fall evenings, after homework was completed and the dinner dishes put away, we would often hike the short distance to one of the ponds and fish until darkness made it impossible to see our lines.

On Saturday nights I would routinely drop them off at the Comfort Theater, where they joined newfound friends to view the latest Walt Disney double feature. On several occasions we traveled to Austin, where country singer Willie Nelson welcomed them to sit onstage during his performances. Sundays, we went to church.

Ashley delighted in the simple exercises of kindergarten, and Anson adapted well to life in a new school, making better-than-average grades, learning to play the coronet in the elementary school band, and priding himself in earning a perfect attendance certificate at school year's end. When summer arrived he took his place in right field as a member of a Little League team sponsored by the local Texaco station.

Jana would call occasionally, and the boys delighted in hearing from her. I, meanwhile, responded to each contact with great apprehension. Though there was every indication the boys were happy and comfortable in their new environment, they clearly loved their mother, and the possibility that they could suddenly be persuaded to return and live with her played constantly in the back of my mind. She, after all, was the one who still had legal custody, and I routinely felt a great sense of relief after every telephone conversation ended.

In time, however, my worries waned. Gradually, after two years, I convinced myself that she realized the boys were healthy, happy, and well cared for in their new world. The unspoken bitterness I had once felt toward her faded.

It was, however, quickly refueled one early spring afternoon. I was at my typewriter, trying to complete my day's writing before the school bus delivered the boys home, when a call came from the elementary principal.

"Mr. Stowers," he said, "your son's mother is here and has asked that we let Ashley out of class to see her. I've explained to her that you are the only one who has the authority to—"

I didn't wait for him to complete his sentence. "I'll be right there. Under no circumstances let my son leave the school." I also asked that he call over to the nearby building where Anson was in class and alert them that he was not to be released to his mother.

During the fifteen-minute drive into town the old, forgotten anger returned. It had been months since Jana had even so much as called, and now, suddenly, she had appeared without notice to, what? Take them away?

As I pulled into the parking lot and made my way toward the school, I saw my former father-in-law, a large, humorless man, step from a car and walk in my direction. That he was a party to whatever was going on infuriated me. Pointing a threatening finger at him as I walked along the sidewalk leading to the school office, I yelled, "The best thing for you to do is get your ass back in the car and stay there."

He glared at me for several seconds, then, without a word of acknowledgment, turned back to the parking lot.

Inside, I found Jana sitting in a waiting area, wearing a colorful spring dress and smiling as if her sudden appearance was nothing out of the ordinary. "I'm here to take my boys home," she said.

"Like hell."

She had, I told her, made a long trip for nothing, and I angrily suggested she leave immediately. As my voice rose, the principal interrupted. "I think," he suggested, "it would be better if you took this discussion elsewhere."

We walked out to the parking lot where we were joined by

her father. I had not spoken with him since we visited shortly after Jana and I had separated. He and his wife, genuinely concerned over our failing marriage, had asked if there was anything they might do to help bring some positive resolution to our problems. They wanted, they insisted, to hear my side of the story. But after I had truthfully explained what I judged to be the cause of the problem, her father had angrily told me to leave his house and not return. He did not want to hear my horrible lies.

Yet I found myself suddenly turning to someone for whom I had lost all respect, hoping that he might lend some reason to the moment. I recounted my endless attempts to explain away Jana's unkept promises to the boys, of forgotten birthdays and repeated calls I'd received from bill collectors asking where they might find her. And, as his daughter stood silently at his side, I described the life Anson and Ashley had enjoyed since coming to live with me; their achievements in school, friends they had made, of the local Episcopal priest's training them to serve as acolytes, and their excitement over the Shetland pony we'd recently purchased. They were happy and doing well and to disrupt that would be criminal.

"Whether you believe me or not," I said, "no longer makes a shit to me. That's all in the past. But I am going to tell you one more thing that I want you to think about while you're driving away from here.

"The Brown County sheriff called me recently, asking if I knew where to locate Jana. It had something to do with bad checks. I told him I didn't have a clue where she might be. I lied for her; for the boys, actually. But I'm goddamn sure not going to do it again."

With that I turned to face my ex-wife. The self-assured smile she'd shown upon my arrival was gone, replaced by a cold, angry stare.

Before I could say anything more, her father placed an arm around her shoulder and began directing her toward the car. "Coming here," I heard him say as they walked away, "was a mistake."

I stood alone in the parking lot for some time, watching their car disappear down the street, wondering what the bizarre scene just played out had really been about. Perhaps Jana had genuinely wanted the boys back. If so, her method had been uncommonly tawdry. Too, I found it strange that she had arrived so unprepared and given up so easily. Was it possible the whole thing had been nothing more than some manipulating grandstand performance, a charade for her father's benefit, played out in the knowledge that I would not agree to her taking the children?

As I pondered the questions a new calm swept over me. Whatever control my ex-wife had held over my life had, in those few moments of confrontation, finally been exorcised, and I bade it a hearty good riddance.

Months would pass before I heard from Jana again.

THE EFFECT OF A DIVORCE on children is difficult to measure. Certainly it is unsettling, a violent departure from the life they are born into and grow to accept routinely as the natural order. At the time my marriage ended, Anson and Ashley were, I assumed, too young to grasp the complexities of adult problems.

My attempts at explanation were superficial at best, made only on those rare occasions when questions about the divorce would arise: People just grow apart . . . their interests change . . . for a multitude of reasons they no longer make each other happy.

The explanations, I knew, were far from satisfactory. Though it was never specifically mentioned, I was sure the boys felt I was the one responsible for the breakup of our family. I had, after all, been the one who left home. Yet I saw no point in trying to explain who had filed for divorce against whom. The truth, I felt, would benefit no one. Time had come for Jana and me to put the past and angry accusations aside and accept the fact that we were still parents, both loved by our children.

I knew the boys missed their mother, but the feelings never seemed to dominate their daily lives. There would be times, however, when the fact would manifest itself in subtle but telling ways.

In a celebration of one Mother's Day, first-grade students were asked to write letters to their mothers with the promise that the local paper would publish their notes of appreciation. I knew nothing of the assignment until the weekly *Comfort News* arrived and I read, *Dear Mother, I love you very miuch because you cook very good dinners. Love, Ashley Stowers.* That evening I had them phone Jana to let her know they were thinking of her.

And it had been later that same year when Anson was to perform in the school's annual band concert. It was to be a milestone in his young life, and he clearly wanted his mother to be there to share in it. "Call her and invite her," I urged.

On the day of the concert, both boys arrived home in great anticipation of their mother's visit. They stepped from the school bus, eagerly asking if she had arrived. They were noticeably disappointed that she had not yet made it. "She'll be here," I told them. "Go get your showers so you'll be ready." In truth, I felt only slight confidence in my assurance.

Too many times in the past, after promising a visit, she had not shown.

After Anson had called to invite her to his concert I had waited until he and Ashley were asleep and telephoned her myself. "This is important to Anson and he's really counting on you being here," I explained. "They both are. Are you going to make it?"

"Of course," she replied. "Didn't he tell you that I told him I would?"

I fought back the urge to remind her of the time she'd also told him she would come for his birthday, but not so much as a greeting card had arrived. "The boys look forward to seeing you," I said before hanging up.

Late in the afternoon, a couple of hours before the scheduled concert, Jana phoned to say she was in town and suggested taking the boys to dinner before going over to the high school. I drove them into Comfort, where we met their mother and a man I didn't know at the local restaurant. I quickly excused myself, saying I would see them later at the concert and inviting them out to the house for coffee afterward.

I was purposely late getting to the high school auditorium, taking a seat in the back, far removed from Jana, Ashley, and the man who had accompanied her. On stage, the Beginners' Band performed a medley of simple tunes in a manner that only admiring parents could appreciate. For Anson, dressed in dark slacks, a white shirt and tie, his shiny cornet to his lips, it was a proud moment.

Afterward, the boys directed their mother and her friend to the house, where I had coffee brewing. They gave Jana a tour of their room and updated her on things they had been doing while her friend—a doctor, he told me—and I sat at the kitchen table making talk so small as to be a waste of the breath it demanded.

In less than an hour they were on their way, leaving behind two young boys made extremely happy by their visit.

Long after they were gone and the kids were asleep, I sat in the darkened living room, sorting my feelings. For the boys, I was happy that she had come; for myself, I was pleased that I had felt neither jealousy nor anger over the fact she had brought a "friend" with her.

Comfort, with its gentle, carefree lifestyle and warm acceptance of a bachelor father and two sons, had provided a marvelous healing ground.

In the years to come, however, I would learn that deep, invisible wounds remained. They would finally reveal themselves in the steadily growing anger of my elder son.

Four

THE TASK OF pinpointing the place and time at which a person's life turns toward a certain direction is, at best, difficult. Early warning signs are overlooked, minor but telling transgressions often forgotten or dismissed. During the three years spent in Comfort, I saw nothing to warn me that Anson was any more troubled than the average twelve-going-on-thirteen-year-old kid.

Does one look back on an afterschool incident when Anson and his best friend conspired to shoplift a pack of cigarettes from the local drugstore and, in retrospect, nod knowingly and judge it the first of many antisocial acts to come? Or does he simply recall the fact they were caught red-handed by the matronly store owner, who immediately reacted with her own brand of old-fashioned punishment and lesson teaching? In exchange for her promise to keep their bungled attempt at thievery secret, they had willingly spent an hour sweeping the floors, dusting the display counters, and washing glasses behind the ancient soda fountain.

For both my sons, the country life, with its simple pleasures and limited demands, was rich with the ingredients for a happy childhood. "It was," Anson would tell me years later, "the only place where I never felt any pressure."

It was a place I, too, hated to leave.

But after three years of modest income earned primarily from all-too-sporadic sales of magazine articles, making a living had become a growing problem. *Recession* was at the time an unpopular but often-used word in the American vocabulary, and it was taking a dramatic toll in those areas of the publishing business I had come to depend upon.

Thus, when the editor of the *Dallas Morning News* Sunday magazine phoned with an offer of a staff position, I weighed it seriously, then reluctantly informed the boys we would again be moving.

The move to Dallas, however, was not the only change that Anson and Ashley would be forced to contemplate. Several months earlier I had met an attractive divorcée named Sandy Sikes, and we had begun seeing each other regularly. She would occasionally come out in the evenings and join our fishing trips and began inviting us to her home for weekend dinners. When finances permitted and a baby-sitter was available, Sandy and I would drive over to Kerrville for a movie and Mexican food. An avid bird watcher, she began to teach the boys how to identify the various species that populated the region.

I welcomed the unexpected return of adult companionship to my life. An avid reader, Sandy was eager to discuss books and favorite authors; she enjoyed music of all kinds—including the plaintive ballads of Willie Nelson, which I favored—and seemed not to mind that much of our time together was spent in the company of the boys. They liked her, I sensed, signaling an approval to our relationship that pleased me.

In time, she and I began to discuss the possibility of marriage, casually nibbling at the edges at first, then gradually moving to more serious discussions. We agreed that for a time the single life had been a welcome escape for both of us. She had been divorced for five years; three had passed since my marriage had ended. Each of us had begun to weary of the loneliness.

Thus when I determined that it would be necessary to leave the Hill Country for Dallas, she informed me that she would like to accompany us.

"Are you proposing?" I asked in mock surprise.

"Well, I'd rather you did," she replied.

Soon after I'd officially accepted the job in Dallas and located a house, we were married in the St. Barnabas Episcopal Church in Comfort.

It was a decision we would both come to regret.

DETERMINED TO KEEP the urban lifestyle at arm's length, we moved to the small community of Cedar Hill, a half-hour drive south of Dallas. With its picturesque town square, a good school system, and a population of less than three thousand, it was as close to the setting we had left as could be found inside the boundaries of Dallas County.

In the first year, everyone seemed to adapt nicely. Anson, preparing to enter junior high, surprised me with the announcement that in addition to playing in the school band he planned to try out for the football team. Ashley made friends quickly and involved himself in the activities of the elementary school. Sandy admitted brief bouts of homesickness for the verdant countryside we'd left behind, but her days were soon filled with gardening, putting a new home in order, and a variety of community activities.

Though I missed the freedom of working at home, I enjoyed now having a weekly paycheck and company benefits.

Then, shortly before Anson turned fifteen, the picture began to darken. As if the idea had suddenly come to him in a vision, some lightning bolt awakening, he adamantly began to argue that he was adult enough to make his own decisions, that rules and obligations were his to determine. Adult authority, on the home front or at school, became his mortal enemy. And he fought against them with a vengence.

His schoolwork fell off to a point where he was no longer academically eligible to participate in extracurricular activities. He became openly hostile to even the slightest suggestion of discipline, and frequent short-term disappearances became routine. My response was always the same: telephone calls to friends he might be staying with or who might have seen him, drives to areas where I thought he might have gone. And the results of such escapades became frustratingly predictable. After exhausting places to stay, he would return, offering a cursory apology and little, if any, detail about where he had been or what he'd done during his absence.

The time-tested punishment of "grounding," tried repeatedly, proved totally ineffective.

One Sunday evening, following Anson's return from a weekend disappearance, I said nothing as he entered the house and proceeded to his room. While he awaited my standard outburst, I went into the backyard instead and, with a sturdy length of chain I had purchased from the hardware store, locked his motorbike to a post, then returned to confront him.

"You get it back when you prove to me that you've earned the right." I was determined the bike would sit idle for some time.

Anson, lying on his bed, looked nonchalantly up at me from a book he had begun to read and said nothing. It was, as always, that blank-faced lack of remorse or the slightest demonstration of concern that routinely ignited my anger.

"Where the hell have you been?"

"At a friend's house."

"I've called all over town."

"I guess you don't know all my friends," he replied sarcastically.

"Well, whoever they are, you can forget them for a while," I shot back, frustrated in the knowledge that, as usual, I was getting nowhere. "Beginning tomorrow, I take you to school and I pick you up. You don't go anywhere I don't take you."

He had already returned his attention to his book before I had completed my last sentence.

The following morning, as I entered his room to wake him, I found his bed empty. Outside, the chain had been sawed from his bike and lay tangled on the ground. Anson was again gone, leaving me to begin another workweek with a fist-size knot in my stomach.

So routine had his runaways become that I reached a point where I was not unduly worried for his safety. Instead, I viewed them only as outrageous displays of defiance for which I could determine no good reason.

Three days passed before I received a midday call at the office.

"I'm in jail," he said, the hostility and anger replaced by the voice of a frightened kid.

"Where?"

"In Duncanville." He explained that police in the nearby community had picked him up in a wooded area of a city park where he'd been camping out for the past few days.

Only when I arrived at the police station did I get a more detailed story. A patrolman alerted to Anson's presence in the park by people who lived nearby had found him asleep in a bedroll and had arrested him.

"The lady who called said her house had been broken into while she was away," the officer explained, "and food items had been taken from their refrigerator and pantry." When Anson was picked up at his makeshift campsite, the officer had found a small cache of snack foods and canned goods.

So clouded was my reaction by embarrassment and anger that I paid little mind to the mental process that would prompt such outlandish behavior and was, instead, relieved to learn that the woman from whom my son had stolen had decided not to file charges.

I picked up Anson at the jail, tossed his bedroll into the backseat of the car, and drove toward home in chilly silence. I was at a loss for anything to say, and Anson, tired, dirty, and suddenly frail-looking, slumped in the seat beside me, staring at the floor-boards.

Only when we reached the house and he began to open the car door did I speak. "Wait a minute," I said.

For the first time he looked over at me.

"The only question I have right now is why."

Anson shrugged. "I don't know."

"Son, I've got to have a better answer than that. But not right now. I want you to get cleaned up, get some sleep, and we'll talk when I get home from work."

We went into the house, where I recounted to Sandy my conversation with the police officer. "Maybe this has scared him enough to straighten up," I suggested.

She did not immediately respond, then said, "I wish I could say that it will." My wife had already given up hope, and I could find no good reason to blame her.

That evening, en route from the office, I detoured by the park where Anson had been found. Why I went there, what answers I hoped to find, I do not know. In truth, I was likely buying time before facing the dreaded confrontation that I knew awaited at home.

For some time I walked among the manicured shrubbery and tennis courts and softball diamonds; I watched as small children, accompanied by smiling parents, happily played on swing sets and seesaws. I entered the bordering woods where I searched briefly for Anson's hiding place. Unsuccessful, I returned to a bench and watched for a while as a family of ducks glided lazily across a small, glasslike lake, searching for visitors with bread crumbs to share. I sat there, pondering the mysteries of my son's life, until darkness drove me away.

Later, I would find no more satisfactory answers at home than I had in the solitude of the park. Anson, shaken by his encounter with the police, was properly apologetic and promised improved behavior. But he would not offer even the slightest hint of what had driven him to such action.

Despite my hopes, I knew that the calm would be short-lived, nothing more than a temporary respite until the arrival of the next crisis.

It was not long in coming.

The cashier of a local convenience store telephoned to alert me that he had been cashing checks for small amounts. I learned that Anson had laboriously practiced forging my signature, then had taken a book of blank checks from my desk.

I began to suspect strongly that he had become involved in drugs, yet his denial was adamant. "Then tell me what you've been doing with the money," I demanded. He refused an explanation.

It was, however, not long before my suspicions were confirmed. On a Saturday night I was awakened by the sound of his voice and went into the living room, where I found him seated on the couch, fully clothed, talking in a slurred voice. I stood in the darkened room, listening as he spoke in monosyllables mingled with occasional laughter. Moving closer, I sat down beside him. "Anson, what are you doing?"

He looked over at me and smiled nonchalantly. "Just talking with the dog," he said. But there was no dog in the room.

For the remainder of the night I sat up with him, anxiously waiting for the effects of whatever he'd taken—in this case, I later learned, paint thinner he'd been inhaling—to wear off.

The following Monday morning we drove to Dallas where I

enrolled him in a drug rehabilitation program, and during his first interview, he admitted to the counselor to whom he was assigned that for the past several months he had been smoking marijuana and using speed.

The new disappointment I felt was mixed with a great sense of relief. With the problem out in the open, perhaps a solution was now possible.

During the next several months the weekly visits to the rehab center seemed to have a positive effect. Anson's behavior gradually improved, I detected none of the signs of drug usage that I'd been educated to watch for, and I began to feel a growing confidence that life might eventually return to normal.

Such was not to be the case.

SCHOOL HAD LET OUT for its annual Christmas holiday, and despite a dread of the season that I had developed in recent years, I found myself embracing the festive atmosphere. This year, I was convinced, the annual chore of negotiations about where the boys would spend their time had been easily resolved.

Their mother had moved to nearby Arlington to live with a sister and had regularly phoned to say that she would drop by to say hello to Anson and Ashley or take them for an early dinner. Several times they had visited her on weekends, and all had seemed to go smoothly. Whatever bitterness I had once felt toward her was finally beginning to fade.

The boys and I had spent an afternoon in search of a native cedar to serve as the family tree, chopped it down, and returned it to the house, where it soon glowed with lights and tinsel and handmade ornaments Sandy had crafted. There was the delightful secrecy that accompanies the wrapping of presents, enticing smells from the kitchen, and excited talk of upcoming parties the boys planned to attend.

The last time I'd spoken to Jana, we had agreed that the boys would spend Christmas Eve at home, allowing us to exchange gifts, have the traditional turkey dinner Sandy had planned, and then attend midnight mass. Then, on Christmas morning I would drive them to Arlington, where they would remain with Jana until the school holiday ended.

It was an arrangement that seemed to please everyone, particularly the boys who, in essence, would have the opportunity to celebrate Christmas twice.

The plan was still in place when Jana telephoned one afternoon to say she'd been out doing last-minute shopping and would like to stop by and take the boys out for a Coke.

As they climbed into her car she had smiled, wished Sandy and me a merry Christmas, and promised they would return in "an hour or so."

When they were not back by nightfall, I knew something was amiss, and I began calling the number where Jana was living. There was no answer.

"You don't think there's been some kind of accident?" Sandy asked. "Or, maybe we misunderstood her when she told us when they would be back . . ."

"She's not bringing them back," I said, the joy of the season melting away into a sick rage.

Sandy stood watching in silence as I began to pace.

It fell to Anson to telephone with an explanation later that night. "Hi, Dad," he said, attempting to affect a casual tone of voice.

"Where are you?"

"We're at Mom's," he replied. "She wants us to spend the rest of the Christmas holidays here."

I made a concentrated effort to hide my anger from him. "Let me talk to your mother."

There was a lengthy silence before he returned to the phone. "She's busy right now," Anson said in a guarded tone. "She said she'll call you later."

I knew damn well that she wouldn't. I also knew that I would not ever again be lulled into the false sense of security that had allowed the devious, well-planned event to take place. Placing a call to a lawyer who had been recommended to me, I detailed the situation. It was time, I explained, that I seek legal custody of the boys.

"Are you sure this can't be worked out some other way?" he asked. I again heard the litany of legal warnings that had been given to me back at the time of the divorce. "Things like this can get pretty ugly."

"They already have," I replied sarcastically. "Are you interested in the case or not?"

It was, he explained, very unlikely that he could get a court order that would get the boys home before Christmas. On the other hand, he saw no trouble finding a judge who would demand their return before school resumed. "Are you concerned that the boys might be in any kind of danger?"

"No."

He agreed to take the case. "We'll get the paperwork under way now, asking that they're returned to your temporary custody immediately after the holidays. Then we'll go to work on making it permanent." He paused for a moment, then continued.

"There's something you need to know about me. If I get into one of these things, I play hardball. And I expect my client to do the same. That's the only way to win."

I was, I assured him, fully prepared to do whatever was necessary to finally bring a resolution to the ongoing problem.

"In that case," he said, "we're going to get your children back for you."

What remained of the Christmas season was a misery as the frivolity and family spirit were drained away. I was unpleasant to be around and wished only for the calendar to move forward quickly, past the no-longer-cheerful carols and lights and presents that I knew would remain beneath the tree, unwrapped by those who were absent.

In more rational moments I tried to fathom the motive for Jana's behavior. Had my decision to remarry, introducing another woman into the daily lives of the children, suddenly become some kind of motherly threat I didn't understand? How, in the name of all things logical, could she feel they were better off with her—a person without so much as a home to call her own and no job?

And for the first time in my life I felt real disappointment in my sons. Certainly they were young and impressionable. And there was no question of their love for their mother. But even their affection and immaturity could not excuse what appeared to be a willing acceptance of something they had to realize was accomplished by lie and deceit. Neither had ever expressed to me any desire to return and live with their mother, yet the pull she continued to exercise on them was almost magnetic.

I wrestled with emotions wound and tangled: I was angry, I felt betrayed, and, above all, I worried that there was a chance that, after all these years, I might lose them to a situation I was convinced could not be in their best interest.

Their fate—and mine—would soon rest in the hands of some judge whose name and face I didn't even know; someone who knew nothing of me or my new wife or my sons and the effort we'd spent forging ourselves into a family.

After years of attempting to conceal my negative feelings for their mother, of silently ignoring her increasingly strange behavior and making excuses for her unkept promises, the time had come for me to make them aware that I was finally ready to put up a fight.

When they returned home a week later I made no secret of my plans. "I'm not going to ask who you would prefer to live with," I said, "because the law states that until you reach a certain age you can't make such a decision for yourself anyway. So, as the adult here, the decision is mine. For a lot of reasons, I believe it best that you continue to live here. And that's why we're going to ask a judge to make it official. Any questions?"

They both meekly shook their heads.

To break the tension, Sandy rose and smiled. "If this meeting is adjourned," she said, "there are presents still under the tree that need to be opened."

With that, life returned to normal.

IN TIME, however, the upcoming custody hearing became my obsession. I phoned my attorney's office repeatedly, seeking advice on any preparations I might make. I contacted friends who agreed to serve as character witnesses and kept a running list of notes on points I felt were important to make when I was called to testify. Old, competitive juices were flowing, and on occasion

I found myself questioning a possible loss of perspective. Certainly, the objective was to win—but not for the simple sake of victory. What I was doing, I continually reminded myself, was what I considered best for the boys.

Still, within the boundaries of the courtroom, success goes most often to the best prepared, most aggressive competitor. Nowhere is gentlemanly behavior less rewarded than in the halls of justice.

On the evening before the hearing was scheduled, I sat in my office for some time, pondering a move I had spoken to no one about, not my lawyer or even Sandy. It was, I knew, important that the judge see the boys' mother in an honest light that was not blurred by well-timed smiles or tears or varnishing of the truth.

I finally reached for the phone and dialed the number of the Brown County sheriff, a boyhood friend, who had contacted me on several occasions in an attempt to learn Jana's whereabouts so he might issue the arrest warrant for the bad checks she'd written.

"Are you still looking for my ex-wife?" I asked when he answered.

The warrant, he acknowledged, was still waiting to be served. "You know where she is?"

"Not exactly," I said, "but I can tell you where she will be at ten o'clock tomorrow morning." I then gave him the location of the Dallas courtroom where the custody hearing was scheduled to take place.

Whether the fact that Jana was arrested the following day, in full view of a clearly surprised judge who was preparing to call his court to order, had any effect on his ultimate decision, I can't say. He did, however, make no secret of his displeasure at having to postpone the proceedings while Jana waited at the Dallas County jail for bail to be arranged.

As deputies escorted her away, my lawyer turned to face me, a look of surprise on his face. There was the faintest trace of a smile as he leaned my way and whispered. "Jesus," he said, "I thought *I* was supposed to be the sonuvabitch here."

THE HEARING was mercifully brief. For the first time in my life I sat in a witness-box, sworn to answer truthfully questions posed me. I described the lifestyle to which the children had been exposed since coming to live with me: Cub Scouts, Little League, school and church activities. The judge was informed that family friends, a member of the clergy, the principal at the boys' school, and my employer stood ready to testify.

When Jana took the stand, her lawyer ineffectively attempted to deflect the court's concern over her financial problems, the fact that she could not even provide a permanent address, and her reasons for originally relinquishing custody. His heart simply wasn't in it.

I was glad when it finally ended. Though it had taken less than an hour, it had seemed an eternity, a wrenching, ugly experience I hoped never to relive. I was glad the boys had not been required to be in the courtroom.

And even when the judge announced his decision it was not over. Though he granted me temporary managing conservatorship of the children, it was only while a court-assigned social worker gathered additional information for a report on which he would base his final decision.

In the months that followed, all parties, including the boys, were interviewed by the social worker and required to make a series of visits to a court-appointed psychologist. I resented the entire invasive process, hated the fact that it continued to disrupt our lives, and wished for it to be over.

As one who had long held a skeptical view of the psychiatric profession, I resented the manner of questions posed me. ("How do you feel about the way your children interact with their mother?" "Do they get along with their stepmother?" "As a child, what kind of relationship did you have with your parents?") What business was it of this stranger with his soft, singsong voice so filled with condescension? How, in a few carefully timed forty-five-minute sessions did he expect to learn enough about me or my family to pass judgment on something so important that it could affect the rest of our lives?

While I made every effort to answer his questions truthfully, wary of the power awarded him by the judge, I despised his intimidating prying and was glad when the sessions ended.

I was not alone in my feelings. The boys dreaded the visits. And even Sandy, more open-minded toward the concept of counseling and the good that might result from it, resented its being ordered by the court.

ONE AFTERNOON I received a call at the office from my attorney. "Your ex-wife's lawyer contacted me," he said, "and says she has an arrangement she'd like for you to consider."

"What's that?"

"She relinquishes custody of Anson. He stays with you. In exchange, she gets Ashley."

I couldn't believe what I was hearing. My patience with the process had long since run out. I was tired of judges and case workers and shrinks and lawyers cast in the role of King Solomon. The idea of separating the boys, of making a choice of one or the other, was absolutely absurd.

"Tell them to screw themselves," I said. "The boys are a set, which I have no intention of breaking up."

It was a conversation I never shared with either of my sons.

Finally, on June 15, 1977, six months after the legal process had been set in motion, I was granted legal custody of my children. The court order provided Jana a weekend visit once a month, specifying a time they would be returned home. The judge, my attorney said, was prepared to order that she make child-support payments if I wished. I didn't. I was just glad to have it over.

Months would pass before Jana would take advantage of her visitation rights. The next time she saw the boys, she told them that she was planning to be married.

HINDSIGHT plays the most evil of tricks. Long after the custody fight had ended, I pondered its effect. Given the circumstances at the time, it seemed the only right thing to do. But while relieved to have the issue resolved, I was keenly aware of the toll it had taken. Though I tried to convince Anson and Ashley that I felt no animosity toward their mother and sincerely wished to see their relationship with her resume free of old tensions, the scars were evident. And I had been a party to their making. My taking legal action had brought into the open many negative feelings I had spent years guarding. Though the judicial system had spared them the weighty responsibility of having to choose between their parents, they were keenly aware of the line that had been drawn. They also were forced to come to grips with the fact that whatever love or kinship that had once existed between their mother and father was forever gone.

It would be years later, well into their adult years, before either would speak honestly of that time. Ashley remembers it as one of the most painful experiences of his life. "I hated it," he says. "For some reason, I felt that it was all my fault, that I was to blame for all the angry things that were being said. I didn't understand everything that was happening, but I remember thinking that it was all because of something I'd done wrong."

Anson's recollection is more callous: "The thing that really bugged me about it," he says, "was having to talk to all these people—social workers, the psychologist—who I didn't even know. I kept asking myself, What damn business is this of theirs?"

Which is to say that in some ways, at least, he and I shared a bond during the experience.

In the months after the custody resolution, he began to slip back into old, destructive habits.

His teachers began calling regularly to express their concern for his lack of interest and effort. "Anson isn't a troublemaker," one told me. "He doesn't cut up in class and isn't disrespectful. The fact is, I like him very much. But nothing I do gets his attention. I pass out tests, and while everyone else works, he stares out the window until it's time for him to turn in a blank paper. I give homework assignments and he refuses to do them. I ask him why, and he just shrugs and says he doesn't care about school. He's bright and capable, but he seems determined to fail."

It was only a slight variation of the reports I'd begun receiving from other teachers. When I would question him about his refusal to do his assignments he would offer me no better explanation than what he'd given in class.

Sandy and I tried to help him with homework; we urged his teachers to provide more regular reports of his progress and discussed the merits of hiring a tutor who might help him along. I warned of the possibility of having to repeat a grade, of the cheerless possibility of summer school classes. Nothing got through to him. He hated school but could offer no real explanation why.

Midway through the ninth grade, he was expelled after instigating a series of fights in the schoolyard. Seemingly unaffected by the two-week dismissal, he began talking of not returning at all. "I'm not getting anything out of it," he argued. "I don't care about school. Going back would just be a waste of time."

Sandy and I replied with all the standard parental arguments, attempting reason before making demands. Again our efforts fell on deaf ears. "I'm not going back," he insisted, turning to walk away.

All patience exhausted, I grabbed him by the shoulders and roughly pinned him against the wall. "I'm really tired of your bullshit," I yelled, my face just inches from his. "You don't run things around here, so you might as well make up your mind to deal with it. Am I making myself clear?"

Surprised by my outburst, he could only nod acknowledgment.

"You're going to go to school, like it or not. If you fail this year, you can just prepare yourself to take the grade over the next. I'm not asking you to like it. I don't *care* if you like it or not. I'm just telling you that you're going to do it."

My tirade had reached full bore: "Keep up the stinking attitude you have right now and things are just going to get rougher for you down the road." I reminded him of his thefts, his drug use, his brief stint in juvenile detention. "I don't want to see you behind prison bars someday. I'm not going to let that happen if there's any way I can prevent it. But, the truth of the matter is, it's up to you."

Even as I spoke my enraged piece, I knew that some dramatic change would be necessary for Anson to succeed academically. Public school was not the answer to whatever problems he was unsuccessfully dealing with.

The following day he accompanied me to the office of a man named Norman Amps, the headmaster of a small private school that was within walking distance of our house. Anson sat with a surly look on his face as Amps outlined the unique aspects of his Whitehall School, the small enrollment, individual attention provided each student, an atmosphere that encouraged the involvement of everyone.

While a member of the staff showed Anson through the classrooms and around the grounds, Amps, a burly, bearded Australian, insisted that there was hope for a youngster like my son. "Some kids," he said, "just don't fit into the social structuring of public schools. I've known a lot of Ansons over the years. Most of them eventually find their way. Here, I think we can help your son find his."

He agreed to find room for Anson in his classrooms.

For a time, I thought it might work. Gradually, Anson's hostility toward the idea of yet another new school began to disappear. His grades, while not spectacular, improved. He seemed to like Amps and his small staff of teachers and even made new friends, whom he began to invite home. As the school year neared an end, it appeared that another crisis had been fought back. He was going to graduate to the next grade.

That all changed on the afternoon I received a call from Amps, asking that I come to his office as soon as possible.

"We have a difficult situation," he said as he nervously paced the room, a man suddenly concerned with the possibility of lawsuits and unfavorable publicity. One of the female students, he said, had returned from the noon lunch break and informed a teacher that Anson had lured her into a storage building on the edge of the campus and threatened to rape her.

Though my son had begun to develop an interest in the opposite sex, I found it impossible to think he might commit such an act.

"I've spoken with both of them," Amps said, "and, frankly, I don't know what to believe. She's insistent that Anson told her he was going to rape her. He adamantly says no such thing occurred."

"Was the girl hurt in any way?" I asked.

"No." She had told him that she ran from the building before anything happened. "But, you can understand that it is most important for all concerned—the girl, your son, and the other students at the school—that we get to the truth of the matter as quickly as possible."

He appeared even more nervous than when I'd first arrived. "What I suggest is this: Since both insist they're telling the truth, I'd like for each of them to take a polygraph test."

"Have you discussed this with the girl's parents?" I asked.

"Her father is coming by when he gets off from work," Amps replied.

I told him that I wanted to speak with Anson before making any decision on the matter.

"I hope you understand the need for an expedient resolution to this," he reminded me as I rose to leave.

"I understand," I assured him. "I'll be in your office first thing in the morning."

As I drove toward home, praying that the accusation was without merit, I was convinced of but one thing: There had to be more to the story than the school officials knew.

That evening, as we sat at the kitchen table, dinner postponed and Ashley sent to a neighbor's to play, Anson listened in silence as I told him of my conversation with Amps.

"She's lying," Anson said. "We went into the storage building to smoke a cigarette, that's all. Sometimes, at lunch, kids go down to this little ledge that overlooks the road and smoke. Other times, we go in the storage building. It's never locked. That's all we did: smoke a cigarette. When Mr. Amps called me into his office, I thought that's what it was about. Then he started asking me all these questions about trying to rape somebody and sent me home."

I tried to impress upon him the serious nature of the charges the girl had made. There were questions I had to ask and honest answers were very important. Did you try to have sex with her? "No." Did you touch her? "No." Did you say you were going to rape her? "No." Even in a joking way? "No."

I explained that the headmaster had suggested that he and the girl each take a polygraph test to determine the truth. "Would you be willing to do that?"

For several seconds Anson searched my face from across the table. "I've got a question," he finally said.

"Okay."

"Do *you* believe me?"

I wished at that moment that he could understand how badly I wanted to tell him that I did, that all the lies of the past were forgotten, that they lent no weight to the issue at hand. But I could not be certain, and thus measured my response carefully. "Anson," I said, "I *want* to believe you."

He shrugged, masking any disappointment he might have felt at my answer. "I'll take the lie detector test," he said, "but she has to take one, too."

On the following Saturday morning, a well-known Dallas polygraph examiner read the results of the test he'd administered to my son and told me that he had found no evidence of deception. "Your son is telling the truth," he said.

Eager to share the news with Amps, I phoned him at home. The news brought a quick sound of relief to his voice. "I'm sorry that it was necessary to put you and your son through this," he said. "Please tell Anson we will see him Monday morning."

"Have you heard the results of the girl's test?"

There was a noticeable pause before his answer. "I'm afraid," he said, "that her father decided against allowing her to be tested."

If Anson had regained any degree of self-confidence or enthusiasm for school prior to the event, it was quickly destroyed by the unjust handling of the episode. When, upon arriving at school, he learned that his accuser had been allowed to return without punishment, he angrily voiced his feeling of betrayal to the headmaster.

And again he began talking of quitting. "I'm not going back there," he said.

I could not blame him for the way he was feeling. When I sought an explanation from Amps, he pointed out that there was no legal way he could dismiss the female student from the school without threat of litigation.

I was furious. "So she gets away with accusing a sixteen-year-old kid of threatening to rape her."

"It is her word against his."

I exploded. "Not according to the goddamn polygraph test."

"I'm very sorry," he said.

In the years to come, I would reflect often on the event, coming to view it as one of my greatest failures. A long history of falsehoods had fueled my hesitation to believe Anson, to immediately rally to his cause at a time when he desperately needed a champion. I had heard "wolf" cried too often to jump immediately to his defense. My support, then, had not been spontaneous and undoubting, and Anson, I'm sure, knew it. And though he has not mentioned it to this day, he was, I'm certain, grievously disappointed by my reservation.

Things spiraled downward from that time forward.

TWO DAYS AFTERWARD, Anson again disappeared, leaving behind all intentions of finishing the final two weeks of the school year. It took only a few phone calls for me to locate one of his schoolmates who was willing to share a conversation he'd had with my son earlier in the day.

"All the kids have heard about what happened," he said, referring to the unfounded charges. "Some people were kidding him about it—just joking around, really—and he got into a fight with some dude. Then he walked off."

"Where was he going?"

"I don't know for sure," the youngster said. "All he said was that he hated this whole town and was getting out of it."

I went to his room and found that clothing and a few personal items were missing. At the foot of his bed was a hastily written note. "Don't try to find me" it read.

Anson had run away, not just from the cruel chiding of his peers or the embarrassment of a classmate's accusations, but also from a multitude of problems and pressures he'd come to judge unbearable.

Our home life had become less than happy. The added responsibilities of a new assignment to the *Dallas Morning News* sports department, covering the Dallas Cowboys, had created the necessity for far more travel and longer, less-predictable hours, and Sandy had become highly vocal in her resentment. Angry shouting matches had become routine.

And I found myself standing between wife and sons, hoping to somehow make everyone happy and failing miserably. I felt as if I were attempting to dig a hole in dry sand.

In the summer, when time had come for me to travel to the Cowboys' summer camp in California, Sandy had made it clear that she had no intention of watching over Anson during my six-week absence. Thus I had taken him with me, but only after a night-long harangue in which he refused to embrace the idea. He had a girlfriend he'd recently become enamored of and preferred to stay at home so he might spend time with her. I literally had to force him into the car to accompany me to the airport.

Such were the battles that were being fought regularly. While I had hoped things might get better, they only got worse. Sandy's unhappiness grew as did her determination to recapture a life of her own. Soon she was venturing on weeklong bird-watching trips to the Gulf Coast, visiting family in Germany, and vacationing with her parents, seeking peace that no longer existed at home. At the same time, her increasingly frequent absences always left behind a brief but welcomed quiet.

Everything seemed to be falling apart. My only recourse was to deal with one crisis at a time. All too often, it was Anson who received my attention.

THE LONG-DISTANCE CALL had come from Comfort, and when first hearing the voice of Herman Roark, I assumed an old friend had simply phoned to stay in touch. He and his wife, Clara, and their sons had spent a great deal of time in our home when the boys and I had lived in the Hill Country. Richard, the oldest of their three boys, had been Anson's closest friend.

Quickly, however, I realized the call was not social. "Anson's here," Herman said.

I felt an immediate sense of relief in knowing that he was among friends and was not altogether surprised at the destination he'd apparently chosen. He had done what all of us, young and old, attempt at some point in our lives: Confused, angry, and disappointed with the world in which he was living, he had returned to a place of fond memories.

"Is he okay?"

Herman hesitated before answering. "He's all right," he finally said, "but he's got some problems."

I was already mentally determining how long it would take me to drive to Comfort when Herman continued. "Anson has stolen a pickup," he said. "That's how he got here. We talked with him for a long time before he admitted that it wasn't yours. The sheriff's on the way over now."

He then handed the phone over to Anson. The Roarks, he told me, had persuaded him to turn himself in. "I guess I'm going to jail," he said, an attempt at bravery evident in his voice.

"Anson, why?"

"Dad, I just got fed up," he said. "I had to get away from everything and everybody." He explained how he'd left school in the middle of the afternoon and returned home, knowing no one would be there at that time of the day. "I packed some things and walked over to the highway and started thumbing."

He had hitchhiked south, reaching the city of Belton just before nightfall.

"I stood on the road for a long time," he said, "but couldn't get another ride. It was getting really cold, so I walked down to a parking lot and got into this pickup. I saw that the keys were in it so I started it and turned on the heater. After a while I decided to steal it."

The next time I saw him was in the Bell County Juvenile Detention Center, locked in an upstairs cell of a musty, decaying old jail in downtown Belton. He was eating a bag of potato chips as I approached.

"How long am I going to have to stay in here?" he asked. There was not the slightest sign of the remorse I had hoped to see.

Nor was my reply what he had wanted to hear. In an earlier conversation with the juvenile authorities they had indicated to me that they were prepared to offer Anson a one-year probated sentence, but only if I agreed to have him committed to the Adolescent Drug Abuse and Addiction Service facility in Vernon, Texas.

"There," juvenile probation officer Lee Todd explained, "he will not only receive intense therapy for his drug problems, but counselors will also attempt to help him work through whatever social problems he's dealing with." During the treatment he would be allowed no contact with anyone outside the facility.

"How long will he be expected to stay?"

"Six months, maybe longer. A lot depends on his willingness to work within the program."

I asked his professional guess of the success such a stay might have on my son.

"Mr. Stowers," he said, "Anson is a very angry young man."

His tone was far from encouraging, but my decision did not take long. If in the process of being punished for the theft of the pickup he could get help for his drug usage, which I feared had not only returned but grown worse, it offered another chance—however slim—of something positive.

"I've signed the papers," I told him.

I drove home dejected, Anson's disappointed expression fresh in my mind. He had, I knew, expected me somehow to engineer his freedom. Instead, he was admitted to the Vernon Center on the last day of November 1979.

LESS THAN TWO MONTHS later I received a letter from the director of the facility. "This is to advise you that a decision had been reached to discharge your son, effective immediately. During his residence here he has exhibited no motivation to change, nor has he cooperated or participated according to the rules set forth by this facility. His attitude has been one of indifference and uncaring about his treatment program."

Anson would, the letter concluded, be released to my custody as soon as I arrived to pick him up.

"What do we do now?" Sandy asked, her question posed with a mixture of resentment and anger. The intrusion of Anson's troubles had, I knew, drained away the final remnants of her patience.

And it had, effectively, helped to bring about the destruction of our marriage.

"Well, I go get him," I replied, no more pleased with the idea than she was. Nor with any real idea of how to deal with the days ahead.

UPON HIS RETURN, we coexisted in an uneasy peace for a time. Anson, still showing no interest in school, began working at a fast-food restaurant, later moved to a car wash, and then was hired by the owner of a lumberyard.

Almost six months passed before he was back in trouble. He stole a car for a joyride that ended when he was involved in a fender bender a few miles away in the neighboring community of Midlothian. The car he had collided with was being driven by the daughter of the local chief of police.

Arrested, he was placed in Woodlawn, a minimum security Dallas jail for young offenders, and immediately escaped by climbing out a third-floor window and sliding down a drainpipe. For two weeks he was on the run, living with friends willing to hide him, before being rearrested.

On September 9, 1980, he was, at age seventeen, convicted of auto theft, sentenced to ten years probation, and returned home for one last time.

Five

THOUGH HE WOULD not talk about it, Anson was having problems with his girlfriend. The signs were always the same: He had become sullen and silent, quicker to anger and rebellion than usual. And there was little I could do to help him.

One evening, after he'd excused himself from the dinner table having barely touched the food on his plate, I followed him into the backyard.

"Want to talk about it?"

He shrugged and looked away, as if to signal the fact he didn't welcome my intrusion into his private misery. But, finally, he spoke. "She wants to break up," he said.

No human pain compares with the agonies of young love, whether real or perceived. There was no anger in his voice, only a genuine aching hurt for which I knew there was no immediate relief. Nor would any advice I might offer provide an acceptable remedy.

While I had watched his romantic relationships from a distance, it was not difficult to detect a familiar behavioral pattern.

"Maybe you just need to give her a little room," I suggested. "Don't pressure her." It occurred to me that I was sounding as if I were borrowing from the clichés of a teen advice column. Yet I had seen Anson's smothering, possessive approach to every new relationship in which he had become involved. He would phone the girl constantly, as if needing hourly assurance they were still "together." He would collect photographs of her into a shrinelike arrangement on his dresser and jealously worry when he did not know where she was and what she might be doing. To Anson, there was no middle ground, no concept of a casual, friendly relationship. He fell in love with each new girlfriend.

"When I was your age," I said, "I did some of the same things. And, boy, I got dumped on more times than I can remember. I could never understand it; never learned. But, looking back, I have to believe that it was because I was more serious about the relationships than my girlfriends wanted to be. And, you know, they were right. We were too young. What I should have done was relax and have more fun."

Anson only nodded, then shoved his hands deep into the pockets of his jeans and turned to go in the house. I watched silently, so wanting to do something that would salve his pain while, at the same time, realizing the impossibility of my wish. What I saw was a boy, struggling with the complexities and confusions of adolescence, badly wanting to be loved.

That which I tried to give was not enough.

At the time, in fact, I was about as poor a role model for good relationships as one could imagine. I had reached the decision to file for a divorce. It had been an agonizing process, long in the making, and complicated by the fact I had met someone else.

I'm sure that anyone who took notice of the attractive and energetic woman who had volunteered to assist me in coaching the local youth track and field program during the summer would point to her as the reason for my seeking an end to my second marriage. More true, however, would have been the fact that I was looking for something I could justify as an excuse. Had not Pat Cruce come along, providing a strong and worthwhile reason for leave-taking, I would likely have continued—for how long, I don't really know—to endure a marriage that had been ill-fated, strained, and generally cheerless almost from the beginning.

Traditionally, there is the obligatory assignment of blame in such matters. Right or wrong, I chose not to dwell on it. Sandy and I had, I felt, both made an effort to enrich each other's lives, at times succeeding. Ultimately, though, the effort had become too weighty a chore for both of us. I had known for some time that the marriage, a too hasty union of people weary of living alone, of singularly shouldering the burden of daily responsibilities, was a mistake. Rather than resolving our respective problems, we had only compounded them.

The strain had begun to show almost immediately.

That my job demanded a certain amount of travel during which she was left to care for the boys soon became an ongoing irritant. Never a follower of sports, she could not understand my inclination to coach Ashley's peewee football team or rise early on Saturday mornings to open the local gymnasium for daylong grade school basketball games in which he participated.

One evening as she prepared dinner before I was to drive to nearby Duncanville to report on a high school football game, Anson entered the kitchen to ask if a friend could spend the night.

Sandy quickly turned from what she was doing. "You're going to the ball game with your father," she said in a sharp voice.

Puzzled, Anson looked at me as if to remind me that he'd already turned down the invitation that I'd earlier extended. With an eye motion, I waved him from the room.

Routinely, the boys had friends over to spend the night, and I didn't understand Sandy's reluctance to allow it on this occasion. I explained that neither Anson nor Ashley had expressed any desire to go to the game with me.

"They're going," she said, her voice filled with hostility.

Suddenly defensive, I asked why.

She turned and hurled the porcelain cup she was holding across the room. The sound of it shattering against the wall preceded her answer: "Because I'm not your damn baby-sitter."

Such shows of temper had become uncomfortably commonplace. Patience exhausted, I found myself drawn into shouting matches, too often in front of the boys. Routinely, these arguments would end with Sandy driving off in anger or hiding away in the bedroom with the door shut.

There came a time when the arguments began to bound on the absurd. As family pressures mounted, Sandy once paid a two-week visit to her brother, a military doctor stationed in Germany. Before leaving, however, she had given me a lengthy list of instructions on the care of her vegetable garden. An avid fan of fresh vegetables and canning, the space she devoted to the project had grown annually to the point where it daily required hours of her attention. Though far less enthusiastic about the rigors of hoeing weeds, watering, and fertilizing, the boys and I were recruited to help.

Each evening during her absence I religiously hosed down the producing plants, harvesting the ripe tomatoes, green beans, and squash, all the while muttering to myself that her once-small garden had taken on the excessive dimensions of a truck farm. She argued that the efforts would provide cost-saving food in the oncoming winter months. My response was a reminder that the romantic pioneer days had long ended. I enjoyed fresh vegetables as much as the next guy but also was sure that I could provide for the necessary groceries even after the temperatures began to fall. Which is to say I had begun to look on the ever-expanding garden as a colossal pain.

Upon her return, she hurried to the garden area and immediately launched into a tirade. I had not watered enough here and too much there, weeding had not been properly tended, vegetables had not been picked at the proper time. She railed about the hours of backbreaking work she had put in, only to see it ruined by my indifference and inferior gardening abilities. "This," she shouted, "will cut in half the amount of things I had planned to can."

She stormed toward the house, leaving me standing in the shambles she perceived.

Instead of following her inside, trying to make peace, I drove to the Farmers' Market in downtown Dallas. There, in an angered frenzy, I purchased large quantities of every vegetable in sight—a bushel of this, a crate of that—until the trunk and backseat would not hold another tomato or ear of corn.

Returning home, I silently proceeded to pile my purchases in the middle of the kitchen while Sandy remained in the bedroom, the door shut to signal the fact that I was not welcome to enter.

Only later did she emerge to find my ill-tempered handiwork. "What is this?"

"I just wanted to make sure we didn't starve," I snapped back in sarcastic, childish fury. "And I wanted to make certain I don't ever have to set foot in that goddamn garden again."

For a moment she glared, then again retreated to the bedroom, slamming the door behind her.

In fairness, there had been some good times. Finally, though, the negatives just seemed to suffocate the positives, draining away the final reserve of emotional energy. In time we just ran out of gas.

Sandy had tried to adapt to the role of new stepmother. And, perhaps, I had expected more of her than I had a right to. The responsibilities of caring for Anson and Ashley deprived her of the independence, freedom, and solitude she'd enjoyed in her single life. In time I came to feel a strong resentment, sometimes spoken, sometimes more subtly expressed, for which I had no solution. I had taken the boys with me as often as I could, freeing her from parental responsibilities that had clearly begun to tax her energies. And Anson, who had seemed to like Sandy initially, became openly defiant soon after we were married. In time, he openly resented the fact that Sandy repeatedly held his younger brother up as an example of the behavior she expected from him.

When possible, I worked from home or slipped from the office early to be available for the daily demands of transportation from school, to team practices or visits with friends. And when I was away, traveling with the Cowboys, I began to carry with me a growing sense of guilt over leaving, always feeling the need to return home as quickly as possible and play the role of peacemaker—all the while feeling an increasing dread of what awaited me.

I was trying to keep everyone happy and succeeding with no one, myself included. It had become an endless, exausting exercise.

The boys and I moved into an apartment, returning once more to our bachelor ways. For a time, in fact, everyone seemed to feel a long overdue sense of relief. Though they were careful not to verbalize their thoughts, I sensed that Anson and Ashley were pleased with the new living arrangement—as if it were some belated attempt to recapture the more carefree times we'd spent back in the Texas Hill Country.

No longer were they exposed to the piercing verbal bouts that had become such a routine part of my life with Sandy. And she was no longer burdened by the presence of a husband and stepsons who drove her to such levels of anger and frustration.

If the split upset Anson or Ashley, I did not sense it. On the other hand, I was dealing with waves of guilt and anxiety that I did my best to conceal. What I had decided to do, I believed, was right and best for everyone concerned. But that made it no easier.

And so when Anson began to sulk over his own romantic misfortunes, I had no real counsel to offer. And even if I had he would have received it, quite legitimately, with a skeptic's attitude. Many times I imagined his thoughts: *Hell, Dad, you botched your marriage to my mom. Now you're going through the same old crap again.*

Thus, I felt decidedly unqualified to serve up advice to the lovelorn.

What I had not known at the time was that Anson and his girlfriend had been involved in a long-running argument over his steadily increasing drug use. At first she had simply urged him to stop, warning of the legal dangers. The bottom line, though, was that she did not wish to continue a relationship with a drug user, leaving the decision to him. Repeatedly, he had promised to quit and had, in fact, told her that he had stopped. But once too often she had learned that he had lied to her.

Finally, she had broken off the relationship. And when she did Anson vanished.

IT WAS IN late January of 1981, following the breakup with his girlfriend and a series of heated arguments we'd had over his behavior, when Anson again left. On this occasion it had been at my insistence. My tolerance, already badly frayed, was finally exausted when I learned that he had taken a twenty-dollar bill— a Christmas gift—which his younger brother had hidden away in his closet for safekeeping.

Furious at such an unconscionable act, I ordered him to leave.

He'd been gone for several days when, on a Saturday morning, I awoke to find my parking space in front of the apartment empty. Unknown to me at the time was the fact that a book of blank checks was also missing from my desk drawer.

I spent the weekend brooding over the certainty that the new year now promised little more than a continuation of the problems of the old one. Why, when given every opportunity to succeed, did Anson seem to go out of his way to orchestrate his own failures?

Less than a month earlier he'd had a good job, working as a member of a surveying crew. He liked the work, and from all indications his employers were pleased with him. Each morning as I cooked breakfast he sat at the kitchen table eagerly talking about the work he would be doing during the day. It was, he more than once had proudly pointed out, a job with a future. He talked of soon having enough money to make a down payment on a car so that I might be free of the responsibility of getting him to and from work daily.

A few days before Christmas, when I had picked him up he had proudly shown me a $500 bonus check he'd received. He seemed prouder when I made him aware that, after only a few months on the job, his bonus exceeded the paltry one I had received from the *Dallas Morning News*.

I saw in his eyes a flicker of self-satisfaction, of accomplishment. He'd finally outdone ol' dad, and it clearly pleased him. And me. It was, in retrospect, one of the all-too-few moments of genuine optimism I had felt about my son in a long time.

The feeling, however, was short-lived.

Just days later he informed me that he had been laid off, entering into one of his rambling, far-too-detailed explanations, which I immediately recognized as a lie.

The following day I telephoned Pat at the Texas Employment Commission—she had helped Anson locate the job—and asked if she might find out what had happened.

The story she heard was far different from the one he'd told to me.

"He was fired," she said.

"What for?"

There was a brief silence that told me she did not want to answer my question. "Stealing," she finally said. "They really liked him. And they were very pleased with his work. But he apparently was taking tools. Nothing of great value, as I understand. Still, company policy left them with no option but to dismiss him. I'm sorry."

So was I. I was also angry and remained so when I later confronted him about the matter. Once again my hope that he would admit his wrongdoing and accept responsibility for his behavior was met with hostile denial.

Why, he replied, would I never believe him? Why was I always so quick to assume the worst? It was an old take-the-offensive-as-a-defense routine I'd become familiar with firsthand over the years, one that I must admit was too often played out effectively. So desperate was I to believe him that at times I would find myself holding to even the most remote possibility that his version might have some grain of validity. Even when I was intellectually certain that it didn't.

It is a dilemma with which all parents wage an ongoing battle. We simply do not want to believe that our children, raised to abide by the proper social mores, might be liars, cheats, and thieves. And even in the face of the most irrefutable evidence, it is far easier simply to deny than to deal with.

On that weekend as I sat wondering what new demons had driven Anson to his latest act, fearful for his safety and at the same time embittered by what he'd done, I arrived at a decision that gave me little comfort.

I telephoned the police and reported that my car had been stolen.

It was not an act born of courage or anger or revenge. Legal right and wrong had nothing to do with it. Simply put, my energies were depleted, my spirit broken, and out of sheer desperation I had opted to hand off the responsibility for dealing with Anson's behavior to the authority of a third party. I wanted someone else to solve my problem.

"Do you have any idea who might have taken it?" the investigating officer asked.

"My son," I said.

In less than twenty-four hours my car was located, impounded in Baton Rouge.

Anson was again in jail.

After taking my car, he had forged my name to a series of checks for small amounts that he then cashed at various convenience stores. He then stopped by a liquor store and purchased a bottle of Jim Beam whiskey (despite the fact he'd never, to my knowledge, done much drinking).

Fueled by anger and no small amount of self-pity, he had decided that he would drive to Baton Rouge and attend a concert by the popular rock group Styx.

Before leaving town, however, he stopped at the home of one of his friends, a young man named Robert, where he broke in and took a Remington 30.06 rifle, a .12-gauge shotgun, a .20-gauge shotgun, and several boxes of ammunition belonging to the teenager's father.

In Robert's bedroom he left a note: "Hey man sorry about the mess. Tell your dad I am sorry to borrow his gun to do this. But it had to be done. I couldn't live without her. Always, Anson E. Stowers."

He requested that Robert see to it that his girlfriend was given the note. Then, in a strange postscript, he had written the name and number of a detective in the Duncanville police's Criminal Investigation Division. "If he isn't already here, call him," Anson had written.

The note, for all intent and purpose, left the impression that Anson had planned to use the stolen rifles to commit suicide. Such a prospect, of course, was terrifying. On the other hand, it made little sense to me that he would take *three* guns if, in fact, his purpose was to end his own life. More likely, I determined, he had planned to sell them. The message, meanwhile, I saw as a textbook example of his long-standing flair for the theatrical—a sad and misguided attempt to encourage enough guilt and fear to persuade his girlfriend to reconsider her decision.

And I found myself wondering what kind of burglar leaves a note admitting his crime, then gives the name and number of a police officer to call and report the offense to.

Anson, I was reasonably certain, had no intention of taking his own life. And he wanted to be caught.

The latter had been accomplished just south of Baton Rouge. Apparently intoxicated since leaving Texas, he had pulled off Interstate 10 and entered an out-of-the-way Louisiana roadhouse near the community of Gonzalez. Since it was just after 11 A.M., the place was deserted except for the elderly woman working behind the bar. She had served him a drink, then watched in silence as he played a solitary game of pool. Long before he approached the bar and asked for a second drink, she had determined that he was drunk. She suggested it was too early in the day to be drinking so heavily and asked that he leave.

Leaning across the bar, Anson glared at the woman for several seconds, then turned and walked into the parking lot. In a matter of minutes, however, he was back, pointing the .12-gauge at the woman. "Okay, bitch," he said, "now you're going to not only serve me another drink but you're also going to open the goddamn cash register."

As soon as he left, the proprietor phoned the police, and in minutes a high-speed chase was under way as Anson fled northward toward Baton Rouge. After reaching speeds of near a hundred miles per hour, he finally pulled to the side of the highway and was immediately surrounded by half a dozen police cars. Anson stepped from the car, his hands held high above his head.

By early afternoon he had been booked into jail and was being interrogated by Ascension Parish deputy sheriff Dan Falcon.

IT WAS LATE in the day when I finally received a call from Phil Hambrick, a longtime friend and lieutenant with the Cedar Hill Police Department. "We've found him," he said, quick to add that Anson was physically okay.

"Where is he?"

"In jail in Louisiana."

Hambrick immediately sensed my assumption that Anson was being held on the car theft charge. "He's got some pretty big problems," he said. "They've charged him with aggravated robbery."

He then went on to describe a telephone conversation he'd had with Deputy Falcon, relaying to me the details of the robbery and arrest. What he didn't mention was the fact that Falcon had also contacted the New Orleans police, who were attempting to determine if Anson might have been involved in a homicide and a series of armed robberies there. Nor did Hambrick mention an offhand observation the Louisiana deputy had made to him:

"The crazy sonuvabitch was lucky he hijacked the place when he did. If that joint had been filled with its regular customers when he walked in, everybody in the damn place would have pulled a gun on him, and somebody probably would have blown his ass away."

The robbery, I learned, had netted Anson $101.

There is no way to prepare for news that your child has committed a criminal act. No amount of private self-warning or even acknowledgment that such a possibility, even liklihood, exists can soften the blow. How many times during the course of heated arguments had I insisted to Anson that if he did not dramatically change his outlook on life he was going to wind up in prison?

With my warning now almost certain to become a reality, I had to wonder if his latest action was some cruel, defiant act to make my prophecy come true. Or by giving mention to such a possibility had I planted the idea that it was some secret wish of mine, a way of last resort to get Anson and his problems out of my daily life?

My thoughts, of course, were absurd. The harsh truth of the matter was that I had nothing to do with his decision to take my car, steal guns, or commit a robbery. Such actions are light-years removed from anything I might ever consider or condone. If Anson's latest trouble was in some way my fault, I would gladly have reported to the book-in desk and offered to take his place behind bars. I was saddened and disappointed, angry and even embarrassed by what had happened, but I did not feel blame.

All of which did nothing to reduce the knot that had formed in my stomach when I learned of what had transpired in some far-away Louisiana town I'd never even heard of. As I was provided additional details, I found my mood spiraling into a deep depression.

In Anson's possession at the time of his arrest were a number of items that shed light on his activities in the days leading up to his arrest. While they meant little to the investigating officer who itemized them, to me they provided the pieces to a sad, puzzling story.

There was, for instance, a pawn ticket for a fourteen-karat gold ring with a small diamond, still in its jeweler's box—the ring he had at one time no doubt planned to give his girlfriend.

Another pawn ticket was for a camera and a .22 pistol, answering another question that had arisen in recent days. Earlier, my estranged wife had contacted the police to report a burglary that had occurred while she was out of town. Upon her return she had discovered that someone had spent considerable time in the house, cooking and even sleeping in one of the beds. A subsequent search for missing items revealed that her camera and a .22 pistol were gone from the closet shelf. She informed the police that she strongly suspected the uninvited visitor had been my son.

The pawn tickets told me that she had been right. They also explained where he'd spent at least part of his time during his recent absence.

And there had been a card bearing the name and phone number of a known drug dealer. It left me with little doubt what the money he had accumulated had been spent on.

I passed a sleepless night wondering what I should do. There was, apparently, no question that Anson was guilty. Convicted, he could not expect any leniency from the court and would routinely be sent to prison. In one foolhardy sequence of events he had gone from adolescent misdemeanor behavior to the commission of a serious adult crime that promised no second chances, no cursory legal slap on the wrist.

What began preying on my mind were the horror stories I'd long heard about the cruelties and conditions of the Louisiana prison system. Angola, the state's maximum security prison, had a long and storied reputation as a hellhole. True or not, I found myself visualizing the worst. And while I knew precious little about the legal system, it occurred to me that the only real help I might afford would be to explore the possibility of somehow getting him returned to a Texas jail. Anson's numerous violations of his probation agreement would, no doubt, ultimately result in his being sentenced to serve time in the Texas Department of Corrections. While the Louisiana offense was clearly the most serious, he could be prosecuted in Dallas County for the two local burglaries and the theft of my car. So, I wondered, would it be possible that the Louisiana authorities might agree to return him to Texas in exchange for some agreement that he would be sentenced to prison time that was comparable punishment for the crime he'd committed there?

The following morning I visited attorney Mike Barclay and sought his advice. He liked Anson and was clearly disappointed to hear of his latest difficulties. Mike agreed to call Louisiana and learn whatever additional information he could about Anson's situation.

Later that afternoon he telephoned to say that convincing the Louisiana authorities to agree to extradition would be no simple task. "Right now," he said, "they won't even talk about the possibility." His suggestion was to let everyone cool down for a while, then pursue the matter again. In the meantime he would speak with the Dallas County district attorney's office to see if it was agreeable to the idea. If so, the next step would be to assure the Louisiana DA that Anson would receive as harsh a sentence in Texas as might be dealt there. It would, he warned, require a guilty plea by Anson on all counts and call for a lot of legal posturing and paperwork. But he too agreed that it was in Anson's best interest not to pay his debt to society in Louisiana. He also suggested that it would be beneficial to retain a lawyer there who could stay in touch with Anson and assist with whatever paperwork and legal pleadings might be necessary.

"One other thing," he said. "They've dismissed the idea that Anson might have been involved in that homicide or any other robberies."

AS MY FLIGHT began its descent to the Baton Rouge airport, I felt an overwhelming sense of dread. In truth, I had not wanted to make the trip; did not want to see Anson any more than he wanted to see me. What was there to say? My anger and disappointment were still too fresh for forgiveness. And already my dreams had been haunted by the disturbing look of fear I anticipated seeing on my son's face. Likely, he would attempt to mask it with coolness, but it would be there in those piercing brown eyes he'd inherited from his mother. Beneath the false bravado and hostility would be a scared seventeen-year-old kid.

I saw it the moment he was escorted into the dingy visiting booth of the Ascension Parish jail. Though only feet apart, we were separated by a wall of glass, each holding a telephone receiver. In those first few silent moments I felt all anger slip away, replaced by the overwhelming desire to touch him, to pull him close and assure him that somehow, some way, I would make everything all right.

Anson, dressed in an ill-fitting jail jumpsuit, a prisoner's plastic ID band on one wrist, broke the uncomfortable silence.

"I wasn't sure you would come," he said. The observation and the tone with which it was delivered were, I knew, calculated to disarm me. It worked to perfection.

Yet the tiny room that we shared was soon flooded with a tension that refused to ease, lending a new level of discomfort to the stark surroundings. I felt the muscles in my body tighten and a dryness in my throat that made speech difficult.

"You okay?" I asked.

He shrugged. "I guess so."

"I talked with Mike Barclay, and he's suggested hiring an attorney here who can work with him. I'm going to see what I can do about that as soon as I leave here."

Anson only nodded, staring across at me through half-closed eyes, as if determined to send me a message of total unconcern.

"We're going to try to get your case transferred back to Texas," I continued in a lame attempt to promote some manner of dialogue. "Mike says it won't be easy, but he thinks it can be done."

"Whatever . . . ," he replied. Then, after a few seconds of awkward silence: "Look, Dad, you don't have to do this. It's my mess, okay?"

I fought to control the anger that quickly began to burn inside me. I felt the sudden urge to drive my hand through the glass that separated us and grab him, to shake the phony attitude from him. His reaction was exactly what I had expected. And dreaded.

Why, dammit, did he feel it necessary to take the tough convict posture with me? Had his thought processes become so twisted that he was feeling some misguided pride, even satisfaction, in what he'd done? Didn't he realize I could see through it as easily as I had all of his other lies?

My frustration had, in just minutes, again edged toward boundaries that taxed every ounce of self-control at my disposal. I had come to help, and he was turning me away. I had hoped to hear him admit to his wrongdoing, to burst forth with an eloquent apology and promise that some lesson which would magically change his life had been learned. Instead I got bad showmanship. And I felt a sudden urge to get out of there as quickly as possible.

"You need anything?" I finally asked.

He softened somewhat at the question. "A toothbrush and some toothpaste," he replied. "Stuff like that."

"I'll leave some money up front." I rose to leave.

I'd reached for the door when he tapped against the glass, signaling me back to the phone. I put the receiver to my ear as he looked across at me. The toughness began melting from his face, his eyes suddenly moist with tears.

"I guess I'm in a lot of trouble," he said.

"I'm afraid so," I answered, despising the dark truth of my response.

Following the tense, strained half-hour visit, I signed for the release of my car, which was parked behind the jail, and drove to the downtown office of a local attorney who had been recommended to me.

A stoutly built black man in his midthirties, Ben Johnson specialized in defending juvenile offenders. He liked kids, spoke a language they apparently listened to and believed in, and was well respected in the local legal community.

In his small, cluttered upstairs office he questioned me at length about Anson's background and our relationship. While there was nothing in his manner to suggest he might be passing judgment, I had the strong feeling that his questions were designed not so much to determine whether he would take my son's case but, rather, to help him decide if I was someone he wanted to work for.

"Your primary concern, as I understand it, is to get your son out of our fair state and back to Texas," he said.

I nodded and he smiled, relieving me of the need to spell out my concerns.

"That," I acknowledged, "and for him to be represented by someone who will see to it that he is treated properly both in the jail and the courtroom." I was looking neither for an attorney to search out loopholes nor for ways to manipulate the system. Though he made no mention of it, I got the impression Johnson found it surprising, maybe even odd, that I had not once asked about the chances of Anson escaping punishment.

Rising from his chair, he extended his hand across his desk. "I'll go see your boy," he said, "then I'll get in touch with Mr. Barclay."

After writing him a check, I left his office and was halfway down the stairs when he called out to me. Leaning over the banister, he said, "This won't resolve itself quickly, you know. And there's nothing much you can do for now. We'll keep you posted. So go on home and get on with your life."

It was, I'm sure, counsel he'd offered to many distraught parents over the years. Still, I found myself replaying his words over and over in my mind as I drove, physically and emotionally drained, back to Texas—back to some semblance of reality.

Somehow, I was going to do what Ben Johnson suggested.

For my own mental well-being as well as for Ashley's sake, it was important that I find a way to prevent Anson and his problems from becoming my singular focus.

Johnson's message was clear: My input into the care of Anson had, in effect, been reduced to a show of paternal support and payment of lawyers' fees. No amount of worry or fear of the future would alter what was already done.

As I drove into the night, my spirits were finally lifted by the sight of familiar landscapes. And I found myself harboring a guilty secret I would share with no one: I was beginning to feel a growing sense of welcomed relief at the distance that now separated me from my troubled son.

IN TRUTH, there are many hiding places to which one can retreat in times of despair. I've known those who have briefly escaped the cruelties and realities of marital woes or financial misfortune in the false comfort of boozy stupors or cocaine binges. Some talk of suicide they will never commit or dramatic life changes they just can't seem to accomplish. I know of a successful businessman, finally overwhelmed by the pressures of a daily life that he judged no longer bearable, who quietly had his lawyer draw up papers turning all property over to his wife and children, authored a brief letter of resignation to his boss, gathered a few personal belongings into a backpack, and disappeared on a bicycling tour of the United States. Another friend, labeled successful and personable by all who knew him, chose to deal with his own private miseries with a Jekyl-and-Hyde personality change. He would become noncommunicative, leave his work undone, and avoid contact with even his closest friends. Retreating into the cave, he called it.

My hiding place was work.

For reasons I shall not even attempt to explain, some of the most prolific outputs of my writing career have paralleled times of personal crisis.

In the aftermath of Anson's arrest, I tended my newspaper responsibilities by day, then launched into marathon night writing of an as-told-to book I'd contracted to do. No magazine editor's request for a story went ignored. Sleep, which promised frenzied, discomforting dreams, became, for a time, something avoided until exhaustion absolutely commanded it.

To anyone who questioned the furious schedule I'd set for myself, the explanation was the simple need to finance my son's legal defense. In truth, I was reaching out to the welcome distraction that came from focusing thought and energy on the subjects about which I was writing. It was the knot at the end of my rope.

Too, there was my younger son to consider. After my initial explanation of what had happened to Anson in Louisiana, we spoke very little of it. His life continued normally, filled with friends, sports, and school activities. I found myself watching him closely, secretly searching for hints that his brother's situation troubled him more than he was willing to admit, and detected no worrisome signs.

What I saw was an unaffected twelve-year-old, busy with basketball practices and games, science fair projects, skateboarding, and homework.

His interest in sports delighted me, offering a common ground for activities and conversation. I had watched proudly as he won a trophy in the Pitch, Hit and Run competition, cheered him on as he qualified for a trip to Houston to compete against others in his age group in the regional Junior Olympics cross-country championships, and won his first blue ribbon in the city elementary track and field meet. In Anson's absence he had traveled with me on trips to cover football games in places like the famed Astrodome, attended a Super Bowl in Miami, and joined me at the Cowboys' training camp, where he participated in a youth basketball camp overseen by famed UCLA coach John Wooden.

The troubling realities I was dealing with were, at best, puzzles he saw no need to solve. While there were, I'm sure, feelings that he guarded, questions that he chose not to ask, I was pleased that he did not seem to dwell on the family problems.

Only once did I see visual evidence of the pain he felt for his brother. Anson was being held in the Dallas County Jail, and after I'd visited him several times, Ashley began to ask about his well-being.

"Do you want to go see him?" I finally asked.

No doubt harboring youthful curiosity about what jail was like, he said he would. Thinking it might cheer Anson while providing Ashley a worthwhile learning experience, I agreed to allow him to accompany me the following week.

What he saw clearly depressed him. Through the small window where jailhouse visits are conducted, he was able to see the cramped conditions in which his brother was forced to live. As he and Anson talked, their faces pressed close to the glass to overcome the constant roar of noise inside, I watched as Ashley's wide eyes roamed to the inmates behind where Anson stood.

Some lay on bare mattresses while others paced, stepping over fellow prisoners, shirtless to combat the airless warmth created by too many people in too small a space. Loud talk competed with the mixed sounds of half a dozen radio stations. In a corner, a group of older men, their faces masks of boredom, played a card game.

That evening, as we drove toward home, Ashley said little. The visit—a mistake I realized as soon as he had arrived on the floor where Anson was being held—had clearly saddened him.

To my relief, he never asked to go again. In the days to come, Ashley might ask how Anson was upon my return from a visit, but whether right or not, his brother's problems were something we spoke about only in passing.

It was as if we had made a silent agreement that by not talking of such matters we could pretend ignorance of their existence.

Yet, in a sense, his brother's long-standing rebellion and constant brushes with the law had prepared Ashley for this latest event. He seemed to welcome the calm that Anson's absence provided.

Meanwhile, I did all I could to provide a sense of normalcy to our lives.

THE WEEKS FOLLOWING Anson's arrest soon turned into months with little indication that there was any movement whatsoever on the extradition process. The Louisiana attorney elevated avoiding my phone calls to a new art form. His secretary, whose voice had become monotonously familiar to me, had the drill down pat: Her boss was in court, in a meeting, out of town. I would not have been surprised if, just for the sake of some variety, she'd informed me that Johnson had flown to the moon for a long weekend.

Barclay, meanwhile, assured me that he was on the case and had, in fact, spoken with the Louisiana attorney by phone on a couple of occasions to learn what progress was being made. "It's going to take time," he repeated, "and pushing the matter will only alienate those whose cooperation we need."

Things were out of my hands, he reminded me. "Dwelling on it isn't going to help."

In such times, I think, we all look rather desperately for guidelines, some tested formula that points the way through life's dark moments. Some find help in the Scriptures, others in the words of a trusted friend. It is the stock and trade of psychologists, clergy, and self-help book authors.

I found myself privately looking to a somewhat unconventional source, a person who had no idea I was attempting to draw on his rare strength.

I did my best to adopt the mind-set of a man I'd admired and been writing about for years. Tom Landry, head coach of the Dallas Cowboys, had long been a fascinating enigma to me. A quiet, square-jawed man with a tunnel-vision approach to his craft, he was generally regarded as one of the greatest coaches in pro football history. Yet his status seemed to have no effect on the calm, ordered manner in which he conducted his life. Those close to him could detect little, if any, change in the Landry whose early Cowboys teams had been league doormats and the one who later had ridden the shoulders of his players in celebration of Super Bowl championships. I've never known a man who kept his emotions so private and in check, dealing—at least outwardly—with the highs and lows of his profession in the same controlled way. Win or lose, Landry was Landry, and I found his ability to put things in perspective fascinating. "I make it a point not to worry about those things over which I have no control," he had often said to me in answer to some interview question I had posed.

It was a sound and admirable philosophy, but, I would find out, one that was damn hard to live by.

I did, however, find that the snaillike movement of the legal system offered time, which finally began to provide a healing distance from Anson's problems. Once resigned to the fact that I was not going to be able to effect any immediate change in his situation, my life settled into a routine that I found more comforting than anything I'd experienced in years.

With the NFL season over, I avoided the office as much as possible. It was good not to be traveling, not to be constantly on call. I watched Ashley's basketball team play, caught up on some reading, and fell into a routine of taking long, solitary runs in the late afternoon.

And there was Pat, whose friendship had rapidly become a new bright spot in my life.

She had been divorced for five years and was raising sons the same ages as mine. I had been impressed with her even before I knew her name. Her youngest, Andy, participated in the local youth sports programs and had developed a friendship with Ashley, visiting our apartment after school, occasionally staying to brave my latest cooking experiment.

What I had initially admired—and envied—about his mother was the warm relationship she seemed to enjoy with her children. Guy, her oldest, regularly accompanied her to games to cheer his younger brother on. Always with a camera, she took photographs that she would later pass out to the young participants. Clearly, she liked kids and kids liked her.

It was a few days after Ashley had returned a kickoff for his only touchdown of the season when she approached me at the conclusion of an evening practice and gave me a picture of him happily striding into the end zone.

In time we began to engage in brief, get-acquainted conversations. From time to time I would see her at the high school track, where I occasionally jogged. We would run together, talking very little, but enjoying each other's company. In time we began to meet regularly for lunch.

I invented countless rationales for my growing interest in this lovely woman. My marriage, I was convinced, was already a doomed proposition. Once I mounted the courage to end it officially, I had privately vowed never to risk the vulnerability of such a relationship again. I would, come hell or high water, live out the remainder of my life as a sworn and dedicated bachelor.

Such were the mind games I was playing with myself. In truth, Pat was fast becoming much more than a friend.

AT TIMES I felt pangs of guilt, not only for having lunches and occasional telephone conversations with Pat while I was still married, but also for feeling a new sense of relief over Anson's absence. In jail, miles away, he posed no immediate threat to my emotional well-being. He was, at one level, no longer a problem I was called upon to deal with daily, and I found myself embracing the new calm.

In secret moments I even came to cheer the turn of events, finally admitting to myself that I had grown to dislike my own son so bitterly that I wished never to see him again. It was a shameful, disturbing feeling I was careful not to share with anyone. What kind of father, I wondered, could hate his own son?

We corresponded, exchanging letters that said very little. I updated him on minor day-to-day events, kept him informed of any news I had received from the attorneys, and made a concerted effort to avoid being preachy and keep the tone upbeat. His letters rarely offered any detail of what his jail life was like or how he was coping. Instead they were every bit as mundane as mine, occasionally detailing his critique of some book I'd sent him and ending with requests for things like family photographs, a subscription to the Dallas newspaper, more stamps, or small amounts of money to spend on items offered by the jail commissary.

By writing him regularly, I was attempting to coat the guilt I had begun to feel over not visiting him more. In the months that followed my initial trip to Louisiana, I had made but one additional weekend flight down to see him. The short time we had spent talking on telephones through the glass window of the visiting room had seemed endless, at best an uncomfortable experience. Neither of us knew what to say and were both relieved when the visit had ended. Leaving the jail, I felt I had been in the company of a total stranger. The conversation was forced and guarded, devoid of any honest emotion.

It occurred to me that in making the trip I had done little more than carry out what I deemed a fatherly duty. Anson, I felt sure, had sensed it.

Before I could plan another trip, I learned that he had been moved, sent to the Feliciana Forensic Facility in Jackson, Louisiana, where he was scheduled to undergo psychological testing that would determine if he was mentally competent to stand trial. My first instinct was to visit him there. I went so far as to call and find out what the visitation schedule was and get directions to the facility. Then, however, Anson had phoned, and when I mentioned coming to see him he adamantly urged me not to. He would, he said, be returning to Donaldsonville soon. Wait until he was back there, then come.

"This place is nothing but a nuthouse," he said. "You don't want to see it." The picture he painted would haunt me for days.

In the afternoons, he said, he played chess with a patient who had refused to speak a word for over a year. Other inmates spent their days in mumbled conversation with themselves.

"Don't come . . . please," he said.

The scene he described made me physically ill. What, dear God, was my son doing in such a place?

"Are you okay?"

"I'm damn sure not crazy," he replied.

In light of a series of events that had transpired since his arrest—things I would not learn until much later—jail officials had legitimate reason to question his claim.

He had been involved in repeated fights with fellow inmates, his sudden temper exploding into rages at the slightest provocation. When he assaulted a guard he was placed in a restraining jacket and locked in a padded isolation cell for twelve hours.

Then, in late February, had come what jail authorities judged to be a suicide attempt. Alerted by other inmates, they had found Anson lying in his cell, bleeding from a cut on his wrist. At the foot of his bed were brief notes he had written to me and to his younger brother.

Shortly thereafter he was transferred to Feliciana.

There, he insisted to Dr. Theresita Jimenez, a staff psychiatrist, that he had entertained no real intent of committing suicide. He admitted the wound was self-inflicted and the "suicide" notes were written in a simple attempt to get himself moved from the parish prison. "I had to get away from that place," he confided, "and I needed to talk to someone."

From a series of tests and interviews, the Feliciana doctors developed a profile of a frustrated, angry, antisocial patient. Anson, according to their findings, was arrogant and manipulative during interviews. He was boastful and demonstrated no guilt about his drug usage, which he now claimed had begun at age thirteen, when he had started smoking marijuana. By fifteen, he said, he had experimented with LSD, which he liked, and PCP, which he didn't care for. He'd tried heroin a few times but found it too expensive.

Anson spoke candidly with Dr. Jimenez about the effects of LSD: "You see a lot of strange things," he told her. He described hallucinations he had once experienced while driving under the influence of the drug: "I saw cars melting in front of me and telephone poles falling to the ground. It scared me."

He admitted that he had been using LSD heavily for three days prior to committing the robbery in Gonzalez and spoke of strong feelings of jealousy, rejection, and loneliness.

And, the doctors concluded in their reports, he demonstrated an extremely hostile attitude toward his father.

Six

O N A B R I G H T, S U N N Y
March day in 1981, I left
my desk at the *Dallas Morning
News* a few minutes before noon and took a short walk that would
change my life. In the nearby Dallas County Courthouse, Pat and
I stood before a justice of the peace and were married.

We had spent long hours measuring the pros and cons, playing
a version of the half-full, half-empty glass game. I was skeptical,
not about my feelings for her but about the chances of my making
a long-term success of this relationship after two had ended so

badly. Despite her supportive efforts, self-confidence was not something with which I was overstocked at the time.

The idea, real or remote, of another failure scared hell out of me.

Her boys, Pat pointed out, were quite comfortable with the idea of combining our families. Ashley, I knew, liked her. Aware of Anson's problems, past and present, she assured me she could deal with them. The positives, she insisted, far outweighed the negatives.

Then there was the matter of a career change I'd been considering for some time. In recent years, my income from outside writing—magazine pieces and books—had eclipsed the annual salary I was earning as a newspaperman, and I had begun thinking seriously about again turning to full-time freelance writing. Weary of the travel, long hours, and hovering bosses, I wanted to explore writing projects that I felt were more meaningful than daily 750-word newspaper articles. I was almost forty and had made no real professional mark. Too, I had found myself wondering more and more just how, if at all, my career had affected the maze of family problems I'd been stumbling through for years.

What right did I have asking her to enter into a marriage whose financial well-being would depend on the measure of my talents and the ever-changing whims of New York editors?

"If you're trying to talk yourself out of it," Pat had finally said, "you're doing a very good job. If you're doing it for my benefit, you might as well just shut up and go buy me a ring."

Thus, with feet so cold I was in danger of frostbite, I did the first smart thing I'd done in longer than I could remember.

With only my sister on hand to serve as a witness, we were

married. Afterward, we had lunch, then returned to work. Later that evening, we sat in the high school auditorium, Ashley and Andy at our sides, watching as Pat's older son, Guy, was inducted into the National Honor Society.

Sitting there, enviously aware of the pride Pat was feeling, I secretly pondered the fates of our oldest sons, young men the same age. What miracle had she performed that had directed Guy to this treasured moment of accomplishment? And how much had my life's missteps been responsible for Anson being locked away in a jail cell hundreds of miles away?

Even in the most joyous of times, sorrow whispered to me.

ON THE AFTERNOON of November 25, 1981, I was at home alone, working in the office I had fashioned from a small back bedroom, when the doorbell rang. Expecting to see some stranger with a sales pitch, I found Anson standing there, weary-looking but smiling through a stubble of beard. In the driveway I could see a 1979 Oldsmobile that I didn't recognize.

I motioned him into the house.

Questions raced through my mind and lodged in my throat as I looked at him, dressed in an oversize jumpsuit, standing there in the living room as if it were the most normal thing in the world.

"I had to get away from there," he said as if anticipating the question I was unable to ask. "I broke out last night."

The young man standing before me was now an escaped prisoner.

THE PREVIOUS AFTERNOON, following the Donaldsonville inmates' daily visit to the small exercise yard in back of the jail, Anson had slipped unnoticed into a darkened detention cell—the same one in which he'd lain handcuffed and shackeled before his transfer to Feliciana—which he knew was always unlocked unless it held a prisoner. Huddling in a corner, he silently remained there until nightfall.

During his stay, Anson had learned that deputies seldom ventured into the jail area after escorting the prisoners back into the building following the brief late-afternoon recreation period. Only rarely did anyone bother to take a head count.

He had been relatively certain, then, that his absence from the barracks-style jail area would not be discovered until breakfast was served the next morning.

Though several of his fellow inmates had tried without success to talk him out of attempting an escape, pointing out the possible dangers and slim chance for success, they remained collectively silent about his plan and had, in fact, eventually pooled thirty dollars in commissary money to help him on his way.

In truth, it took no great escape artist to accomplish the getaway that Anson carried out. Soon after the lights had been turned off in the jail area, he simply walked down a hall to an unlocked door, which opened to a small parking lot.

Thereafter, luck became the key ingredient.

After checking several cars, he came upon the unlocked Oldsmobile, which was owned by a jail employee. The keys were in the ignition. In the backseat was a jumpsuit; in the glove compartment was a .22 pistol.

Anson quickly slipped the jumpsuit over his olive green jail uniform, then slowly drove from the parking lot, not turning on the headlights until he'd reached a blacktop road that led to the interstate and freedom.

What he had neither counted on nor known about at the time was the fact that a silent alarm had been set off when he opened the back door of the jail, alerting deputies to a possible escape.

As he neared the interstate Anson saw the parked patrol car of a Louisiana state trooper, red and blue lights flashing. The trooper, standing in the middle of the road, was waving his flashlight as a signal to stop.

Anson thought briefly of pressing his foot to the accelerator but abandoned the idea just as quickly. He could, history had already proven, win no high-speed chase. Instead, he slowed and pulled off on the side of the road near the officer.

"What's going on?" he asked in his best effort to appear casual.

"We've had one escape from the jail down the road," the trooper said. "I'll have to check your car."

Anson nodded as the man beamed his flashlight into the back-seat. In an attempt to make small talk, Anson mentioned that he was headed to an all-night restaurant that was visible in the distance.

"Would you mind unlocking the trunk?" the officer asked. Anson stepped from the car, careful to make sure his jumpsuit revealed no sign of the clothing he wore beneath it, and opened the trunk.

In another minute he was on his way.

Not until he had crossed the Louisiana border in the early morning hours did he stop for gas and breakfast on the outskirts of Orange, Texas.

From there he had driven to Cedar Hill, somehow managing to elude both Louisiana and Texas law enforcement, which had been alerted to his escape.

AS THE SURPRISE AT his sudden appearance began to subside, I found myself begrudgingly impressed at his accomplishment. Perhaps it was some sort of distorted fatherly pride, some misguided admiration I was feeling. But, by God, he *had* managed to do what his lawyers hadn't: He'd gotten back to Texas, had escaped the Louisiana system. The additional crimes he'd committed, I rationalized, were a small price to pay. I felt confident that it would now be possible for him ultimately to serve his debt to society in the Texas prison system, closer to home and in a safer, more just environment.

"You've got to turn yourself in," I said. I suggested that we call Mike Barclay immediately so that he might make whatever arrangements were necessary. The proposal was met with a hesitancy that was instantly deflating.

"I've got to think about it," Anson replied.

An old anger I hadn't felt in months quickly emerged. "What the hell is there to think about? They're going to be looking for you, damn it. Don't you think they've considered the possibility that you would come here? This isn't some stupid game; you're in serious trouble. Jesus, Anson, use your head for once."

What had he expected of me? That I would offer a safe hiding place? A grandiose getaway plan he'd not been able to come up with? Some kind of magical help that would make all his troubles disappear? By coming to the house, having just broken out of jail and driving a stolen car, he had placed me in a position of being viewed as a possible accomplice to his actions, and I resented the hell out of it. That my advice was once more being summarily dismissed angered me. And I hated his ability to turn my life inside out with nothing more than a knock at my front door.

"Look," he said, "I just wanted to stop by for a minute. I wanted to see you. But I'll take care of my own problems."

I knew, as surely as we stood there, that he would not be able to do so. And with that realization, my anger collided with an all-too-familiar feeling of numbing, helpless frustration.

Could I, he asked, loan him a change of clothes? "I need to be getting out of here," he added.

I WAS SITTING IN the living room, replaying the brief, almost surrealistic encounter, when Pat walked in. Returning from picking up Ashley and Andy at school, she had a puzzled look on her face. As she had turned onto our street, she thought she had recognized Anson behind the wheel of a car she had just passed.

I nodded, relieved that she and the boys had not been at home when Anson arrived. "He escaped last night."

"Oh, my God," she said, reaching out for my hand. "What are you going to do?"

"I'm going to do what I told him I had to," I said. "I'm going to wait a few more minutes, then call the police."

THE REMAINDER of the day passed in slow motion as I awaited word of the inevitable. The Cedar Hill police, already notified of Anson's escape by Louisiana authorities, had begun searching for him. Mixed with my concern was a certain amount of relief in being able to tell them that I had no idea where he might have gone after leaving the house.

All I really knew was that my son's life was becoming more complicated by the minute. And there was nothing I could do but wait to see how this new dark drama played out.

If he didn't turn himself in, I knew, he would soon be appre-
hended. And I silently prayed that he would emerge from it
unharmed.

It was almost midnight when he telephoned. "I went by to see
Mike," he said.

I felt a rush of relief. "And?"

"He told me the same thing you did: to turn myself in."

"It's the only thing that makes any sense."

"I'm thinking about it."

Barclay's power of persuasion, apparently, had been no more
effective than mine. The lawyer's conversation with Anson had
ended with his loaning my son twenty dollars and telling him that
he would have to telephone the Dallas County sheriff's office and
inform them that he'd been to his office.

"Anson, what are you going to do?"

"Dad," he replied, "I don't want to go back to jail." With that
he hung up. His voice had become suddenly lonely and almost
childlike, filled with the sad, lost sound of undisguised despair.

IN TRUTH, Anson already had a plan.

After leaving Barclay's office, he had driven to a south Dallas
apartment complex in search of a friend who he hoped might help
him sell the stolen car he was driving. The person who Anson
contacted explained that he would have to make some calls and
suggested they talk again the following day.

After Anson left, his friend had immediately dialed the number
of the Cedar Hill Police Department.

POLICE CHIEF PHIL HAMBRICK is something
of an enigma. An enthusiastic student of modern law enforce-

ment techniques who jumps at the chance to attend any seminar that might enhance his knowledge of criminal investigation, he embraces the long hours demanded of his profession. Unlike many small-town police officers, he enjoys a first-name relationship with FBI agents based in Quantico and police chiefs of metropolitan departments throughout the nation. Even in the isolation and relative obscurity of Cedar Hill, he has earned a reputation as a skilled officer who, more than once, has helped solve cases in other cities thanks to the widespread network of informants he has cultivated over the years.

Yet he has never indicated serious interest in climbing the professional ladder to a more high-profile position in a larger department. A man with an affection for the small-town lifestyle, he finds comfort in knowing the people and community he is sworn to serve.

First acquainted through early difficulties I'd experienced with Anson, Hambrick and I had discovered that we'd spent our youths in some of the same small West Texas towns, had mutual boyhood friends, and in fact had both graduated from Abilene High School, though at different times.

Over the years, we had fallen into a routine of occasional meetings for coffee at the local Dairy Queen, where our conversations rarely went beyond the most recent exploits of the Dallas Cowboys or the latest news from back home.

He had been in Abilene for the Thanksgiving holiday when his office contacted him with news of Anson's escape and the tip that he was attempting to sell the stolen car. For Hambrick, it was a welcomed excuse to return home. In preparation for the trip, he'd been forced to board a newly acquired puppy at a local kennel—something he'd never before done—and had worried non-stop about the animal's well-being since leaving.

While Hambrick was making the drive back to Cedar Hill, Anson stayed on the move, driving aimlessly and blending among the holiday shoppers in a busy mall where he met briefly with an old girlfriend. If he was successful in selling the car, he told her, he was going to purchase a bus ticket to Mexico.

In Hambrick's office, meanwhile, another plan was being organized. Since the informant's apartment was located in Dallas, the Criminal Investigation Division of the Dallas Police Department had been contacted. Working in concert with Cedar Hill authorities, they had devised a method by which they hoped to apprehend my son.

When Anson called, their informant was to indicate that he had found a buyer interested in the car and arrange a noon meeting in the courtyard of the apartment complex.

The area would be surrounded by plainclothes officers who would quickly move in when a prearranged signal was given and make the arrest.

As the meeting was breaking up, Hambrick rose from his chair and offered a personal observation to the visiting Dallas officers. "I've known this kid for years," he said, "and his father's a friend of mine. Let's do our damnedest not to get anybody hurt."

Despite the constant urge to do so, I had not been in contact with the police since my phone call to alert them to Anson's visit. Barclay, clearly disappointed that he had not heard from Anson since their initial meeting, had called to assure me there was nothing that could be done until my son was back in custody. Then, he said, he would pursue every legal avenue to dissuade the Louisiana authorities from seeking extradition and allow Anson to be tried and sentenced in a Dallas courtroom.

Ultimately it would boil down to, he explained, the Dallas County DA's office agreeing to seek a punishment on Texas charges that were severe enough to satisfy their Louisiana counterparts. "They're going to have to hammer him pretty good," Mike said.

Thus I found myself in the discomforting position of having to help assure that Anson would be sentenced to a lengthy stay in the Texas Department of Corrections. While the violation of parole and the burglary charges were serious offenses, it would, I was told, be beneficial if I did not request the dismissal of charges on the theft of my automobile. I was involved in one of those judicial catch-22s that so often makes the legal system a raging parody of itself. To do something good for my son, I had to help the local authorities make him look as bad as possible. It was a situation, I knew, that Anson would never understand.

And so, then and to this day, Anson's lengthy criminal record includes charges that his own father brought against him.

I T   W A S   E A R L Y in the afternoon when Phil Hambrick telephoned. "Anson's in custody," he said. "He was arrested about an hour ago and taken to the Dallas County jail."

"Is he . . ."

"He's tired and scared, but he's okay."

Anson had arrived at the apartment complex courtyard at a few minutes after noon and was immediately surrounded by plainclothes officers who had been hiding in bushes and a nearby laundry room.

He surrendered immediately, raising his hands above his head. "I've got a gun," he had yelled out, not as a threat but simply to alert those whose own weapons were pointed at him. A Dallas officer approached and pulled the .22 pistol—the one Anson had discovered in the glove compartment of the car he'd taken in Louisiana—from the waistband of his jeans. The officer then handcuffed him.

It was over in a matter of minutes. Only three days, which had seemed to me like an eternity, had elapsed between the time of his escape and arrest. And I found myself wondering if there had been any part of his brief return to the free world that Anson had enjoyed. I hoped so. It would be a long time before he would again have the opportunity.

I waited until the following day to drive into Dallas to visit him in the county jail, dreading the routine I had come to know by heart. En route, I stopped at a convenience store for a cup of coffee, and as I stood at the checkout counter a headline on the front page of the local paper caught my eye:

ESCAPEE LEADS POLICE ON CHASE AS CRIME SPREE ENDED

For a moment, the fact that it referred to my own son didn't register.

THE ARREST, routine by police standards, would in short order became part of Dallas Police Department legend when a remarkable bit of irony was discovered. The serial number of the gun Anson had been carrying was checked, and it was discovered it had once been owned by the very Dallas officer who had taken it from him at the apartment complex. The officer had sold it in Dallas over a year earlier. How it had found its way to Louisiana and the glove compartment of the car Anson took was never determined.

Even years later, when the bizarre happenstance was related to me, I found no amusement in the dark cop humor that had been passed around in the aftermath of the discovery. "Wouldn't it have been a helluva note," at least one officer had flippantly observed, "if while making the arrest he'd been blown away by a weapon he'd once owned? What are the fucking odds?"

It was something, even in retrospect, I was glad not to have to consider.

THE LOUISIANA AUTHORITIES agreed not to seek extradition, and on January 21, 1982, Anson was sentenced to fifteen years in the Texas Department of Corrections. He was nineteen years old.

Seven

NOWHERE IS SOCIETY'S caste system so blurred as it is behind prison walls. It is a miniature world with few secrets and little privacy, a place where survival is the paramount goal one awakes to each day. Murderers and rapists mingle with dope dealers and breaking-and-entering specialists, militant blacks with racist whites, gays with straights. It is a world wherein the neurotics and sociopaths, the strong and weak, young and old, are judged as one. Angry-eyed men, certain they have been deserted by God, scoff at the repentant convict who clings to the newfound hope of jailhouse Christianity, and hardened repeat offenders skilled at "doing time" harbor precious little compassion for the dry heaves and plaintive midnight cries of the frightened first-time inmates. Genuine friendships are rare, flawed by a wary distrust that quickly becomes part of the grinding, dismal lifestyle.

Many have the constant desire to hide away, to disassociate themselves from the volatile, dangerous world they've been locked into. They pace through the long dark nights, fighting the will to close their eyes until the first gray signs of a new sunrise. Then, if lucky, they can sleep through the horrors that await outside their cell doors in the daylight hours. In truth, however, there is no real retreat, no safe place, no corner of true respite. In time most give up and take their chances in the woe-filled warehouse they've been sentenced to live in, passing the time with menial work in the prison kitchen or laundry, the law library where they search endlessly for some legal loophole that their attorney just might have overlooked, or classrooms where they study for tests that will ultimately provide them the equivalency of a high school diploma.

More often than not, the anger and hostility that constantly simmer cause the good to turn bad and the bad only to get worse.

On each visit with Anson I heard a new degree of anger in his voice. As I sat on Saturday afternoons, denied even the simple act of a handshake by the mesh wire and glass that separated us, I looked into eyes pinched with hostility—not directed toward me as much as at an unforgiving world whose main purpose he felt was to make his life forever miserable. He spoke of cell block fights won and lost, of harassing guards who constantly filed disciplinary reports against him, days and nights spent in solitary confinement as punishment for deeds he deemed inconsequential. There, with only his thoughts for companionship, the anger incubated and grew. Whether he was in or out of prison, Anson seemed blind to the merits of working within the system. Instead, he fought it with a dedicated vengeance, oblivious to the fact that the only person he was hurting was himself.

He liked the solitude, he insisted, because it removed him from those he called the "crazies," inmates who screamed through the night until their voices became little more than plaintive, raspy whispers, smeared feces on the walls of their cells, and prowled the dayroom, offering sexual favors in exchange for a cigarette or a friendly smile.

I came away from each visit drained and despondent. For days the hopelessness and horror of the environment into which my son had been exiled would cling to me, and I found myself wondering what was really being accomplished by my travels to see him.

We talked rarely of anything substantive. His response to my repeated urgings that he make some special effort to avoid trouble and abide by the rules were shrugs and a litany of unkept promises. His message was clear: It was the system that was at fault, not him. The rules he broke were always unfair to begin with, his confrontations always started by some other person.

In time, I began to feel my own anger at his self-serving explanations and arrogant refusal to pass his time as quietly and quickly as possible.

What made it so difficult for him to see that his actions were self-defeating?

Finally, Pat posed an equally difficult question: "Why do you keep putting yourself through this when every visit is so painful?" she asked.

"Because," I responded, "it's what fathers do." Whether out of love or concern, guilt or curiosity, I was not certain.

My explanation, I knew, was a poor one that satisfied neither my wife nor members of my family. Though they had not said as much, I felt certain that my mother and father had come to view my continued support of Anson despite his lengthening list of faults as an exercise in futility. My sister, who had so delighted in playing the role of aunt when he was younger, frankly admitted that she had become fearful of him. My brother seldom spoke his name. And even Ashley had quietly begun to distance himself.

Anson's relationship with his mother had, over the years, evolved into what I viewed as a love-hate proposition. During numerous conversations with me he had verbally lashed out at her, insisting he neither wanted to see nor speak with her. No doubt wearied by his mercurial emotions, Jana too had finally given up.

I could blame none of them. Yet the idea of total family desertion, of his waging his battles alone, saddened me. Convinced that I was all that stood between Anson and complete isolation from family, I felt compelled to stand by him.

Which is not to say my life was consumed by Anson's ongoing troubles. The good times, in fact, had begun to far outnumber the bad.

At times I wondered at the drastic differences between my two sons. Ashley, outgoing and happy, seemed too involved in his own activities for undue brooding over his brother. He had a marvelous gift that generally enabled him to focus on his own life and responsibilities and not dwell on surrounding problems that were not of his making, and it pleased me greatly. Still, though he never admitted it, I sensed a quiet, welcomed relief on his part when Anson was away. The ever-present angst bred by his big brother's presence had been replaced by the long-overdue care-free lifestyle kids are supposed to have.

Ashley busied himself with athletics and other school activities, routinely joined friends at the skating rink on Saturday nights, and seemed happy with his surroundings. The transition into a new family setting had been accomplished without the slightest apprehension. Not only were he and Pat's son Andy best friends, but I marveled at how comfortable Ashley seemed with his new stepmother.

It was, in many ways, the best of times for him and for me.

I had long worried over the effect Anson's behavior might have had on Ashley, but I felt that concern wane as I watched him growing into adolescence. His even temperament and pleasant demeanor were a delight, and I was thankful that our lives had finally been warmed by a sense of well-being.

He maintained contact with his mother, regularly traveling to her home for weekend visits. Aside from those times when the scheduled visits conflicted with a football or basketball game he was to play in or some social function he was hesitant to miss, he looked forward to the visits with Jana and her new family.

In time, however, his enthusiasm for spending the weekends away from home lessened, not because of any wish to avoid his mother but rather because of the perfectly normal childhood enthusiasm for the friends and hometown activities that had become such a routine part of his life.

By the fall of 1982, in fact, gentle nudging was required to see that he continue making regular visits to his mother. While restrictions had never been placed on how often he went, it was agreed that at least one weekend per month should be spent in Belton.

On one such weekend I was scheduled to travel to St. Louis to report on the Dallas Cowboys–St. Louis Cardinals game, and Pat had volunteered to drive Ashley to the designated halfway meeting point. During the drive, Pat recalls, Ashley showed little enthusiasm for the trip, repeatedly voicing his concern for activities he was going to miss. She had gently reminded him that several weeks had passed since his last visit and that his mother missed seeing him.

"It's just for the weekend. You're not going to miss that much."

"Okay," he had replied with a resigned sigh.

Yet by the time I arrived home late on Sunday night a drastic change had occurred. "When I went to pick him up this afternoon," Pat said, "his mother told me he had decided that he wants to come live with her."

My first question was why.

"I have no idea," Pat said. "Ashley really wouldn't say much. Jana was doing all the talking. I did ask him if it was what he wanted to do, and he indicated to me that it was."

I was stunned. There had not been the slightest indication that he was unhappy or had even considered the idea of living with his mother. I tried without success to imagine what could have transpired during the brief weekend to bring about such a change in attitude. If Ashley had a good reason for his sudden decision he refused to share it with me. It was, he repeatedly insisted, just something he wanted to do. "Dad," he said, "I'm not unhappy or mad at anybody. But I've lived with you for a long time, and now I'd like to live with Mom for a while."

A call to Jana, in hopes of some better explanation, was a waste of long-distance charges. I sensed a gloating as she assured me it was "something he's been wanting to do for a long time." He had, she added, simply been afraid to tell me.

During the next couple of days Pat and I wrestled with the situation, hoping to better understand Ashley's sudden determination to leave. We suggested the logic of waiting until midterm, asked how he would feel leaving the football team in the middle of the season, what he would tell his friends.

But, clearly, his mind was made up. And I found myself in the position of keeping a promise I wished I'd never made.

Back during the torturous custody hearings I had explained to him that under state law a child is considered old enough to decide which parent he wishes to live with when he reaches the age of fourteen. "If you want to go live with your mother when you reach that age," I had said, "all you'll have to do is tell me and I'll help you pack your bags."

Which is what I reluctantly did, secretly hoping that he would soon return.

He did, but only for weekend visits and summer vacations. After almost ten years of seeing him every day, waking him in the morning and being the last to tell him good night, I became the visited parent.

For weeks after he left I had a recurring dream in which I would awake to the noise of a door opening and race to the front of the house, expecting to see that he had decided to return home in the middle of the night. Then I would wake, always disappointed. I missed him terribly—missed attending his games, seeing him shooting baskets in the backyard and playing with friends, having him accompany me to the Cowboys practice field.

In time, though, the hurt of his leave-taking eased, and I found myself looking anxiously ahead to those weekends when he would return home—and dreading the time he would again leave.

Still, the question of why he had chosen to leave remained. Was his decision as simple as he had insisted—that he wished to spend more time close to his mother? Had he met a girl and in the short span of a weekend become so infatuated with her that he wished to make the move? Or had something driven him away? Had the long-running turmoil—Anson's problems and my rocky second marriage—just been too much for him to bear? I worried that the latter was the case and agonized over the fact that he had chosen to leave just when our lives had begun to take on a new, welcomed brightness.

When I attempted to talk with him about it, the only reason he ever chose to offer was the one he'd given me originally. He seemed happy and I chose to leave it at that.

In time I put aside the disappointment of his decision and learned to enjoy our times together.

I CAN, IN TRUTH, recall only one trip to see Anson from which I left with any positive feelings. He was nearing the end of his first full year of incarceration when a springtime invitation arrived from the warden's office, announcing that a graduation ceremony would be held for those inmates who had successfully fulfilled the requirements for a GED. My son would be among those graduating.

It was a promising accomplishment, the first step in the right direction I'd seen in ages, and I found myself anxiously looking forward to the ceremony. Pat, aware of my excitement, volunteered to accompany me to the prison.

On an unseasonably warm April afternoon the graduation exercises were held in a festively decorated room that earlier in the day had been the site of morning chapel services. Inmates dressed in starched white prison uniforms were seated in the front, stealing excited glances at family members in the rows behind them. There were brief speeches of commendation from TDC officials, songs performed by a prison choir, and finally, the procession of graduates marching to the podium, each to receive his certificate.

For the moment, the pall and misery of prison life was forgotten in the hot, overcrowded sanctuary. Parents and wives applauded as men of all ages walked hurriedly to the front of the room—many smiling, none attempting to hide the pride of the moment—as they were recognized.

Afterward a reception was held and prisoners were allowed an hour to mingle with visitors, sharing punch and cookies and quiet conversation as their reward. Anson hugged Pat and shook my hand. "I'm glad you could come," he said, a warm, genuine delight brightening his face.

On that afternoon I briefly saw a different Anson, smiling and cheerful, talking optimistically of days ahead, feeling good about himself. I wanted desperately to make a freeze-frame of the moment and have it last a lifetime. But all too soon came the announcement from an attending guard that the prisoners were to be escorted back to their respective units. And in that instant the realities of time and place returned, leaving behind only the sweet, brief memory of the moment.

On the drive home a new kind of sadness swept over me. For some of the men I had seen earlier in the day, burned out and prison weary, decades removed from their high school years, the ceremony had signaled what was likely the crowning accomplishment of their broken lives. For others, young men still clinging to future hopes, the passing of the GED exam had been little more than a means of getting ten days erased from each month they had been sentenced to serve. Still, regardless of motive, they each had, for a couple of hours on a humid Sunday afternoon, been singled out, judged special in a world where few things special exist.

Pat, I sensed, silently shared the same thoughts as we drove toward home through a red Texas dusk and into a bright moonlit night. With little experience at prison visitation, I knew she had approached the trip with silent apprehensions, concerned over what her reactions to entering Anson's world might be.

"I'm really glad I came," she finally said. "I thought it was very nice. Much better than I expected." There was a thoughtful, melancholic quality in her voice that I had rarely heard.

"Well," I said, trying to lighten her mood, "I'll bet it is the first graduation you've ever attended where armed guards searched your car before you could drive it into the parking lot."

She gave me a tolerant smile and continued to volunteer her thoughts. "It's hard to explain how I felt. I realize the purpose of the whole thing was to celebrate something good and positive. And I *was* proud of Anson. And happy for you.

"But, at the same time, I couldn't help but think about what it would be like for him and the others when we left, after the punch and cookies were gone, and the decorations were torn down."

She fell silent for several minutes, then spoke her last reflective words about the trip: "God, it's such a sad, awful place," she said.

I could offer no argument.

IN THE LONG MONTHS that followed, I gradually sensed the birth of a new attitude in Anson. There was less mention of the down side of his daily life in his letters and calls; the self-pity and anger were replaced with talk of enrolling in drafting classes offered by a nearby junior college that participated in the prison's in-house educational program. His days had begun to pass more quickly, filled with work in the kitchen, a regular exercise routine, studies, and reading the paperback novels I mailed to him.

He had also started a countdown to the day he would come up for parole and began to talk of his plans for life on the outside.

I delighted in his newborn optimism and began to contemplate ways that I might help. If in fact Anson was going to weave his life successfully into the complex fabric of society, it would have to be accomplished soon. Too often I had heard stories of petty criminals who became so accustomed to life in prison that they came to accept the strange comfort of its routines. Freed from the pressures of decision making and concern for the financial and social demands of the real world, they embrace the childlike idea of others directing their lives. And, too, there is the time-tested maxim that insists if you are not an accomplished criminal when you enter prison then you are certain to learn quickly while in the company of those who are.

Such were the reasons I, too, began to look forward to the day Anson would be released. I did not want him to become one of those who prison psychologists labeled "institutionalized," spirit and hope broken, willpower erased. Nor did I want ideas of new unlawful acts to take seed.

IN THE SPRING OF 1984, AFTER SERVING almost three years, he made his first appearance before the parole board and was denied release. I shared his disappointment. In a time of great concern for the problem of prison overcrowding, when 80 percent of the Texas inmates were being granted parole on their first date of eligibility, Anson's punishment was prolonged.

During the course of my son's misdeeds, I had never felt justified in arguing with authorities. It was a simple philosophy, inherited from my own parents: If one breaks the rules, there is a price to pay, no questions asked. And so long as that payment is dealt to one and all offenders equally, there is little, if any, room for argument.

This time, however, I could not sit idly by. I felt a powerful sense of urgency to take control somehow of his life, to remove him from the soiled environment he'd languished in for too long.

"I've got to get him out of there," I told Pat.

"How?"

"I'm going to go talk to someone." As a journalist I had become casually acquainted with a man who I felt might be able to help me with my problem.

I SAT IN AN OFFICE decorated with framed and autographed pictures of Cowboys greats, SMU all-Americans, entertainment world celebrities, and nationally known politicians, not at all comfortable with my mission. Throughout my life I had stubbornly avoided seeking the help of others, convinced that life's problems were best kept private and dealt with through one's own best efforts.

Yet there I was with a figurative hat in hand, reaching out to an influential Dallas businessman I hardly knew, hoping he would hear me out. Among those who had his ear, I'd long known, were the overseers of the Texas Board of Pardons and Parole.

I went right to it, explaining the legal troubles Anson had encountered, reviewing the time he'd spent behind bars, and telling him of the recent denial of parole. "I have no problem with the amount of time he was sentenced to serve," I said, "but I believe he's paid his debt."

"You have any idea why his parole was denied?"

In all likelihood, I explained, the fights with fellow inmates and a series of confrontations with prison guards during the early months of his imprisonment had badly blemished his record. "He's hardly been a model prisoner, but I'm convinced the longer he stays, the worse it is going to get. If he's to have any chance of getting his life back in order, he's got to get out of there."

The man locked his fingers and placed them against his chin, as if searching for signs of my sincerity. "It's not going to be easy, you know," he said. "I've been watching guys like your boy for years. Some make it, most don't. You planning to help him when he gets out?"

Anson, I assured him, would receive as much help as my wife and I could provide. I had, in fact, long ago written the parole board, promising that he would live at our home until such time as he was able to afford a place of his own, that I would help him find a job and see that he had transportation. I had also volunteered to take personal responsibility for seeing that he paid his regular visits to whatever parole officer he was assigned to.

"You know," he said, "when all is said and done, it doesn't really matter that much what *you're* willing to do. Or how many people are pulling for him and praying for him or lending him money. Things like that help, but they aren't the most important thing."

I waited in silence for several seconds before he continued his thought.

"See, it's really not your call," he said. "Unless I'm mistaken, you've probably done about everything you can think of. From here on it's up to the boy. He's the one who has to make up his mind that he's going to get along in the world and make something of himself."

That said, he leaned forward and reached across the desk for the telephone, pushing the button that connected him with his secretary. "See if you can get ahold of my friend down at Pardons and Parole," he instructed.

He rose and extended his hand, signaling the end of our visit, offering no explanation of who his "friend" might be. "I hope things work out," he said. "Meanwhile, get in touch with your boy as quickly as you can and impress on him that the most important thing he can do is be sure he keeps his nose clean."

Ten days later, on a sun-bleached afternoon in late August, I answered the phone and heard Anson's voice. "I'm home," he said.

I drove toward the Dallas bus station, pondering how I might repay Anson's benefactor for what he had been able to accomplish with just a single telephone call.

After picking up my son I explained that there was a stop we needed to make before heading home.

"There's someone you need to thank," I told him.

HOMECOMINGS, even under the best of circumstances, are awkward. Expectations of how things will be conflict with the realities of how they actually are. Things so clearly remembered turn out not to be nearly as sharply defined as the mind's eye recalled them. Anticipated familiarity is quickly replaced by a sudden need to acquaint oneself with new routines, new faces, and a new world. To those of us who never left, the change had been so gradual, so subtle as to be no real change at all. However, to one absent for three years, confined to a tiny, colorless world where change rarely occurs, even the gradual growth of a tree or the fact a new fast-food restaurant has opened for business on a once-vacant corner is a jolting departure from time-frozen memories.

Anson drank in his new freedom with hungry eyes and an almost childlike enthusiasm.

In his first days of freedom, he would wake early, sometimes remaining in the bedroom that had once belonged to Ashley for hours before venturing from his prison-acquired yen for solitude. When we were not searching out the job market, shopping for clothes, or looking for a reliable used car, he stood anxiously ready to busy himself. He mowed the yard, raked leaves, volunteered to help with the dishes, and kept his room spotless through constant cleaning. On outings to a neighborhood restaurant he almost gleefully researched the menu before selecting some item long foreign to his taste buds. And the simple joy of an afternoon spent wandering a nearby mall delighted him. "I want to go somewhere I can see people doing what they want to do, not what someone tells them to," he said.

Routinely, he would return home to tell me of the surprising increases he'd discovered in the prices of items ranging from cigarettes to toothpaste and of fashion changes he'd noted in clothing store windows.

It was, I soon recognized, his way of relearning the ways of life on the outside.

I became so wrapped up in Anson's return that for a time I failed to recognize the concern Pat was trying hard to hide. The presence of an ex-con in the house made her uneasy. Though she had said nothing about it, my son scared her.

She knew well his self-destructive background, had been quick to see through his litany of lies, and privately worried over his lightning quick temper. And with good reason.

He had been home only days when we sat in the living room one evening after dinner, watching television. Nemo, the family dachshund, whom Pat adored, had jumped onto the couch where Anson sat. In an instant reflex, he backhanded the dog, knocking it to the floor as Pat looked on in horrified disbelief.

Quickly realizing what he'd done, Anson began to apologize profusely. He picked up the dog, frightened but not injured, and began to stroke it. He looked across the room at Pat and me. "I didn't mean to do that," he said. "I'm going to have to get used to having pets around. . . ."

Pat excused herself from the room as Nemo wiggled free from Anson's grasp to follow her.

"Dad, I'm really sorry," he said.

The incident had stunned me. Anson's action had not, I didn't think, been born of cruelty but rather was an uncontrollable reflex. In a sense it was a microscopic example of the problems that had followed him throughout much of his life. He had simply acted without thought of consequence. The dog, wanting only to be friendly and loving, had been unceremoniously shoved away.

"Things are going to be hard," I said, "if you can't control your temper any better than that."

Anson nodded. "I know," he replied. "What can I do to make it up to Pat?"

"Just don't let it happen again."

While there were no similar incidents in the weeks to come, Pat's wariness, hidden from me, continued to grow. One morning as she entered his room to change bed linens, she discovered a large buck knife on his nightstand and called me into the room.

"I don't want this in the house," she said, clearly upset as she pointed down at the knife.

That evening, when Anson returned home, I instructed him to get rid of it.

"It's legal," he argued. "I showed it to a cop at the mall right after I bought it, just to make sure."

"What do you need it for?"

"Protection, I guess."

"Look," I said, "you're not in prison anymore. There's nobody out here who is going to hurt you as long as you mind your own business. I don't want it around, so get rid of it."

The knife disappeared, but not Pat's reservations. Without telling me, she had visited our family doctor to request a prescription for tranquilizers.

Anson made contact with his parole officer and soon found work with a construction crew that was building a huge new church just minutes from where we lived. In the evenings we would sit in the backyard, talking of the future, weighing the possibilities of taking college courses, discussing budgeting that would ultimately allow him to set up housekeeping in his own apartment.

He seldom mentioned his time spent in prison, as if not reflecting on the past years would erase it from memory. It was, Anson insisted, time for a new start. "I'm not a kid anymore. I screwed up that part of my life. Now it's time to see how I can handle being an adult."

For a time it went well. As soon as the construction job was completed he found employment with a well-established cabinetmaking firm that offered a modest but acceptable salary, insurance benefits, and weekends off.

And he began to date a girl named Annette Robinson.

They had known each other since school days and had become reacquainted when Anson recognized her one weekend as she shopped at the mall. In short order they were spending all their free time together. Blond and petite, china-doll fragile, she lived with her grandmother despite the fact she professed having a good relationship with her parents. Her father, she said, worked as a boat mechanic for Dallas millionaire H. Ross Perot. Though I had no recollection of her when she and Anson were classmates, teachers remembered her as a marginal student, pleasant but constantly given to flights of fantasy. Following graduation she had gone to work as a waitress at a Dallas nightclub.

"I'm in love with her, Dad," Anson confided after a couple of months. They were, he said, talking of finding an apartment to share.

From the day of his return home I had walked a parental tightrope, determined to sidestep the pitfalls that had so troubled our relationship in years past. Though he still possessed trouble-some, immature qualities and too often unreasonable expecta-tions of himself and those around him, I had made up my mind to view him as the adult he had become, not the child I still too often saw. It was, I believed, time for me to let go, to lend advice only when sought, and then in small measure.

The time had come for him to test the waters of adulthood, to venture from the safety and comfort of home. If he wanted to move into an apartment with his girlfriend, I told him, I was ready to lend whatever start-up help might be needed.

I loaned him money for the first month's rent and necessary utility deposits while Pat shopped for needed household items—dishes, pots and pans, silverware, linens, etc.—to help furnish the small but comfortable dwelling they had found.

Moving into a place of his own generated a measure of pride and excitement long foreign to Anson. Annette shared his enthu-siasm for their new surroundings, hugging Pat and thanking her profusely for her help.

One weekend evening, after delivering several bags of gro-ceries as a house-warming gift, Pat and I sat, enjoying our restored privacy, discussing the recent events.

"They seem very happy," she observed.

"You think they'll make it?"

She paused before answering. "I think there's a chance," she replied.

I sensed that she had more to say. "And?"

She reached out and rubbed her hand against my arm, a gentle gesture to assure herself I was hearing what she had to say. "It's time for us to step back and see that they get that chance. They don't need us hovering over them. They know where we are if they need us."

I could only smile at her careful use of the plural, since it was so obvious that her suggestion was directly aimed at me. "Then," I said, "*we* will just have to disappear into the background, won't we?"

She nodded in agreement. "I think it's best."

In the weeks to come, Anson and Annette would stop by occasionally, to say hello or join in a backyard barbecue. They participated in the family Thanksgiving Day tradition of turkey, dressing, and watching football games. And while I was careful not to pry, Anson always made a point to reassure me that things were going well.

It would be early December before I saw the first grim indication that such was not the case.

Anson had telephoned to say he'd decided it was time to take Annette to meet his mother. His car was not running well, he explained, and he was leary of using it for the trip. He asked if they might borrow mine. "We're just going to drive down early Sunday morning and come on back that evening," he said.

The proposed visit to his mother, after his long and bitter assertions that he never wanted to see her again, came as a surprise. Perhaps there had been fence mending I was unaware of; maybe in his efforts to restructure his life Anson had recognized the counterproductiveness of the ill will he had so long harbored against Jana. Whatever the reason, I chose to view it as a positive step and agreed to let him use my car.

Both Anson and Annette appeared happy and upbeat, looking forward to their trip, when they arrived that Sunday morning to get the car. I handed him the keys and a credit card. "Just in case you have some kind of trouble on the road," I said.

By the time they returned late that night things had changed dramatically.

I was watching the evening news when Anson came through the front door without even bothering to knock. Annette stood behind him, a concerned look on her face.

Rising from my chair I walked toward them. "How was the trip?"

"I had an interesting conversation with Mom," Anson spat, old anger echoing in his voice.

"Oh?"

"Yeah," he said, "I learned a helluva lot. Like what a mother-fucking sonuvabitch you really are."

"What are you talking about?"

"You never gave a shit about me, did you? Not for one fucking minute." Standing in the foyer, his anger exploded into an uncontrolled, almost maniacal rage.

Pat, startled by the yelling, came into the living room in time to hear Anson fly off on a rambling, cursing review of myriad shortcomings his mother had assigned to me.

Anson pointed an accusing finger at me as he hurled charges: I had been a horrible husband, a disinterested, unloving father. He spoke of a time when, as an infant, he'd suffered with measles and I had, according to his mother, refused to offer the slightest comfort despite her tearful pleadings. My mission in life, he had finally learned, had been to make her miserable.

His voice climbed to a piercing, wounded pitch as he continued his tirade. "The only person you've ever given a shit about is yourself. You've been a selfish asshole all your fucking life . . . and you make me sick."

As his rage continued I glanced at Pat, who had cupped her palms over her mouth, clearly shaken by the frightening scene playing out before her.

"Look," I said, taking the car keys from his hand, "I don't know what this is all about, but I've heard all I want to hear. I want you to turn your ass around and walk out that door. Right now. When you calm down come back and maybe we'll talk. But never like this again."

He glared, pulled my credit card from his shirt pocket, and tossed it toward me. "Fuck you, . . . Dad," he said before walking out into the night.

Pat slumped into a chair, a stunned look frozen on her face. "I've never been so scared," she said as I tried to calm her. "My God, he was crazy. I was afraid he was going to kill you. What on earth did his mother say to him that would have set him off like that?"

"I have no idea," I said. But I knew that no amount of venom spewed by my ex-wife could be held completely responsible for such frantic behavior. Nothing she might have said could have triggered such unbridled rage.

Pat had not looked into Anson's eyes, had not seen pupils that looked like hard, tiny black BBs.

"He's using again," I said.

I WOULD NOT hear from him again until the day after Christmas, when he and Annette briefly stopped by to announce that they had been married earlier in the afternoon. If Anson had any recollection of our last conversation, he gave no indication or hint of an apology.

In time, however, I would look back on that evening as the first sign that the roller coaster was moving toward another downward plunge. This time, I decided, I did not wish to be a witness to the crash.

It occurred just a few months later.

First, he lost his job. His boss had been "hassling" him, Anson said, so he had quit. Then came the financial difficulties, each spawning some new and remarkably inventive explanation for the need to borrow money: Annette was en route to the grocery store, rent money in her purse, when she was robbed at gunpoint; pregnant, Annette had miscarried and was briefly hospitalized, draining their funds.

The past had been strewn with too many untruths for me to believe the stories Anson told. Throughout his life one thing had never changed: He remained a horrible liar. Hoping to avoid my expressed disappointment and frustration at each new plea for help, he reached out to me only as a last resort. We were, in effect, trapped in a destructive game that we played all too well. Resentful of my interference in his life, Anson longed for independence, yet he could not escape the need for my help. I, on the other hand, wanted badly for him to stand on his own feet and resolve his own problems. But, like Pavlov's dog, I continued to run to the rescue whenever summoned, all the while searching for some method that might be more effective than the last.

Rather than hand over money for overdue rent payments, I began writing checks directly to the apartment manager. Instead of giving out grocery money, Pat accompanied Annette to the supermarket and paid the bill herself.

One afternoon, after a visit to their apartment, Pat had returned, obviously disturbed over what she had encountered. The refrigerator and pantry shelves were again completely barren except for a single can of cat food. Even in the hardest of times, Annette had made certain the little kitten she had rescued from the animal shelter and named Mikey was fed and taken care of. That alone was enough to endear her to my wife.

After another of their shopping trips she returned with news that Anson had disappeared. "Annette says he's not working or even looking for a job," she reported, "and that he's apparently using a lot of drugs. He's been taking the money she's earned and stays gone for days."

Bile churned in the pit of my stomach. "Goddamn him," I said.

There was more: "He's also been beating her," Pat continued. The bruised ribs and broken ankle Annette had suffered weeks earlier had been no accidents, she had learned. Anson, in a fit of anger, had pushed her down the stairs of the apartment.

"She's all alone over there, scared to death, and has no way of getting around. The apartment—you wouldn't believe it—is filthy, trashed out. It's just horrible . . ."

The concern and repulsion I heard in my wife's voice troubled me, and I felt a new level of shame at the actions of my own flesh and blood. That Pat, innocent of anything that might have led to such behavior, had to be exposed to such nightmares was both saddening and embarrassing to me. I had wanted badly to shield her from them and had failed miserably.

"Do me a favor," I said, "and don't go back over there."

"I've got to," she replied. "I told Annette I would help her move her things to her grandmother's house. She's leaving."

Once again, Anson had driven away someone who cared for him.

Somewhere out there, wandering among the flotsam of Dallas's drug culture, he was off on another aimless search. For what? A new hiding place from his dismal failures? The fickle, short-term feeling of well-being found only in crack houses or back alleys?

The warnings of the man who had helped speed Anson's parole began to ring through my subconscious—". . . *it's not your call . . . it's up to him . . .*"—and I found myself regretting having gone to him for his wasted effort—and sharing something in common with Annette.

I, too, was ready to give up.

THE KNOWLEDGE that Anson had been physically abusive to his wife sent my concerns in a new direction. It was a cowardly act of violence that troubled me greatly—one for which I had neither comprehension nor the slightest degree of sympathy. That Anson seemed determined to toss away his own opportunities, fouling his life with self-destructive behavior, was one thing. The scars, both physical and emotional, that he was leaving on others was something else.

Months passed without my hearing from him, and I relished the peaceful silence, suddenly gaining new momentum on the book I was writing. Realizing the long unanswered yearnings I'd harbored for life's gentler routine, the knot in my stomach disappeared and the violent nightly dreams finally gave way to restful sleep.

During those moments when concerns for the whereabouts of

my son crept to the fore, I fought them back like some arch-enemy. *It was out of my hands . . .*

Then late one night came a collect call from the Dallas County jail. Anson had been arrested for several unpaid speeding tickets.

"Look," he said, "I know you don't want to hear from me, but I need some help. I'd stay in here and just work the tickets off, but I need to get home to Ann. She just got out of the hospital . . ."

"You're back together?"

"Yeah," he acknowledged.

I feared an honest answer to my next question. "Why was she in the hospital?"

"She had this cyst on one of her ovaries and it ruptured. She's okay now, but she's still feeling a little weak. I need to be home with her. If I could get you to pay off the tickets—a hundred eighty dollars, I think it is—they'll let me out. I really hate to ask . . ."

Whether it was relief that his legal problems were nothing more serious, concern for Annette's health, or just the same weary knee-jerk response that had marked our relationship for years, I agreed to pay his fines.

"Dad, this time I'm going to pay you back," he said. "That's a promise."

I didn't bother to respond.

The following day I traveled to the jail and paid the fines, but still holding to my determination to keep a distance between us, I didn't stay to see him released. I wanted desperately to break the chain of dependence, but, in truth, I didn't know how. By agreeing to bail him out of yet another problem, regardless of its seriousness, I had once again ignored my resolve and sent a message that I still stood ready to play the rescuer's role. Motivated by guilt and searching for some way to lend help to my son, I was unable to hold to the private vow I had repeatedly made. I could not just turn my back and hope that he might solve his own problems and find his own way. In retrospect, I was doing neither of us a favor.

It was late in the fall, that time of the year when the days had grown shorter, giving way to a late-afternoon twilight that slipped quickly into sudden darkness even before the commuters could make their way home from downtown offices. Night had fallen before the paperwork freeing Anson had crept through the slow-moving jail system.

When arrested he had given all his personal possessions, including his wallet and the small amount of change in his pocket, to Annette before getting into the squad car. Set free without even the necessary quarter for a pay phone call, he began the long walk to his new residence—an east Dallas motel room—he and Annette had moved into.

As he made his way along Stemmons Freeway, the lighted sign outside the mammoth Infomart, a newly erected building housing showrooms and offices promoting the latest in electronic and computer technology, caught his eye. The marquee advertised an upcoming seminar on computerized drafting.

He stood, staring up at the message for several minutes, his thoughts suddenly visited by lost dreams. While in prison he had taken several drafting courses, scoring the second-highest grade among the inmates enrolled. Upon his release, he had applied for numerous apprentice positions around Dallas without success before settling for construction work. But that had been just a job; drafting could have been a career. He briefly pondered the $200 enrollment fee, then, stuffing his hands into his pockets to ward off the night chill, he walked on.

To one who lacked twenty-five cents for a telephone call, it was nothing more than another in a long line of fantasies that were far out of reach.

The reality was that Anson's life had become far too out of control, his thought processes so muddled by chemicals that genuine ambition had become a total stranger to him.

I would soon learn the new depths to which he'd fallen.

Following his reconcilement with Annette they had briefly lived with her grandparents, then moved into a fifty-dollar-a-week room at the Tower Motel, a frayed old white stucco waystation that survived only to house drug dealers, prostitutes, and the downtrodden.

At one time it had been one of Dallas's finest motels, awaiting east-bound travelers on the main highway leading into the city. Ultimately, though, it had been swallowed up by freeways, bypassed by toll roads and a new interstate that afforded motorists faster, easier routes to their destinations. Soon the Tower's new neighbors became foul-smelling liquor stores, strip joints, and X-rated movie theaters.

In the midfifties the city fathers had first been forced to recognize the blight the Tower had become. Vice cops raided the motel, arresting dozens of prostitutes. Newspaper accounts of the raid revealed that the owner of the motel was a coach and teacher at a prestigious north Dallas school. The unfavorable publicity had cost him his job.

Still, the Tower had somehow managed to survive, the centerpiece of a neon no-man's-land that beckoned the thrill seeker in search of cheap sex or a quick fix.

I had, in fact, come to look on the motel with great disdain long before learning that Anson had become one of its inhabitants. Years earlier, while researching a magazine article on the tragedy of the lost lives of teenage runaways, I had heard it mentioned often.

Pimps, always in search of a pretty new face to add to their stables, would prowl the local bus stations in search of young girls arriving in Dallas, fleeing a variety of hometown boredoms. Some—broke, scared, and alone—willingly moved to the Tower, eager to market their bodies from the curbsides of Harry Hines Boulevard. Those who resisted would be literally abducted, shoved into a waiting automobile, and transported to the motel, where they were drugged, raped, denied food and sleep, and held hostage until the idea of prostitution was viewed as their only chance of survival.

Such was the world in which my son had been living for several months, barely functional, existing from one drug-induced high to another. In an attempt to hide his location and identity from curious police or those to whom he was in debt, Anson had paid an aquaintance twenty dollars for a stolen driver's license issued to William Thomas Holland III and used that name to all but those who knew him.

It was as Mr. and Mrs. William Holland that he and Annette were registered at the Tower. Fellow residents knew her as a topless dancer at a nearby club and her husband as an unsuccessful, want-to-be drug merchant with a sour disposition and an ever-present wasted look on his face.

During the five months they lived there, Anson's drug dependency grew to a point where the simple act of getting out of bed on some days was a physical challenge.

Even in the most fogged and desperate bouts of drug usage, however, there are occasional, though brief, flashes of rational thinking, moments when the trapped addict escapes to a safe distance and is provided a vantage point from which to view his own self-destruction.

Late one night, after a lengthy bout with fever and vomiting, Anson had recognized the horror of his situation. He had to get help and began a stumbling door-to-door journey until he found someone who would drive him to the office of his parole officer the following morning. Finally, a neighbor agreed to drop him off on his way to work.

In the predawn of the following day, Anson sat alone on the front steps of the parole office, sick and shivering, awaiting the beginning of the business day. It was hours before he was waved into the tiny office of his parole officer.

There he candidly admitted that he had a drug problem that was out of control. "I'm so strung out that I can't function," he said. "I need some help."

It was a plea the officer had heard often during his brief but overworked career. "Have you talked with your father?"

Anson shook his head violently. "This is my problem, not his."

The officer shrugged. "In that case, the phone book is full of numbers and addresses of rehabilitation facilities that help with problems like yours," he said. "I suggest you contact one of them immediately."

It was a response that should have come as no surprise. In my initial meeting with Anson's young parole officer I had come away with the strong feeling that he had no control over his task. Too many cases and too little experience had already overwhelmed him, beaten him down, and drained all enthusiasm from him—just as it routinely did to so many in his line of work. The stack of case files assigned him literally covered his desk, signaling the impossibility of his assignment. I knew immediately that Anson would receive no personal attention, that he was nothing more than a number on a file folder to the man who was legally charged with the responsibility of helping him redirect his life.

After his plea for help, Anson never visited his parole officer again.

Later in the day he scored some crack, got high, and dismissed as folly the thought he needed help. Going to his parole officer had been a stupid idea, he thought. If he wished to stop using drugs, he could do so whenever he damn well wanted. He didn't need anyone's help.

SEVERAL WEEKS LATER, he was bent over the fender of an old pickup parked in front of his motel room, cursing the truck's dysfunctional engine, when a female Dallas Police Department patrol officer tapped him on the shoulder.

"Your pickup?" she asked.

Anson shook his head. "Naw, it belongs to a friend of mine," he answered. "I told him I'd try to get it running for him."

"Got some ID?"

Anson pulled his billfold from his hip pocket and held the driver's license out to her. If she noticed the amateurish effort to replace the original owner's picture with his own, she gave no indication. "Hope you get it running," she said before returning to her squad car and driving away.

As he leaned under the hood to resume his task, the wrench he was holding slipped from a hand that was suddenly sweaty and cold.

The pickup did not belong to any "friend." It had, in fact, been sitting in a nearby parking lot for days, apparently abandoned. With the help of another resident, Anson had towed it to the motel to see if he might be able to get it running.

A half hour passed before the police officer returned and again called out to him. "Having any luck?"

"Not much," Anson nervously replied.

"Look," she said, "I've been talking to some of the people who live around here. Why is it that everyone calls you Anson? That's not the name I remember seeing on the driver's license."

His only answer was a shrug he hoped appeared non–|chalant.

In her conversations with residents of the motel she had, in fact, learned much more than his real name. Wary of the police, inhabitants of a place like the Tower Motel are quick to deflect questions about their own secrets by eagerly passing along information about others.

The officer was now asking questions to which she already had answers. "Where'd you get the truck?"

A resigned look on his face, Anson idly began gathering his borrowed tools, wiping each clean on the grease-stained remnants of an old T-shirt as he pondered his answer. "It's just an old, abandoned truck," he said. "Nobody else wanted it."

"So you stole it," the officer said.

Anson knew it was futile to argue. "Yeah," he said, "I guess I did."

———

ON JANUARY 7, 1986, Anson stood before a district judge and pled guilty to charges of auto theft and parole violation and was sentenced to three years in prison.

Once more, Pat helped Annette move back into her grandmother's home.

Eight

TEXAS WAS in the midst of its 1986 Sesqui-centennial celebration, a year-long breast-beating marathon designed to make the rest of the world sit up and take note of the fact that the state was, at age 150, still as spry and full of brag-gadocio as ever.

We were well into a 365-day series of events marking the milestone: a horse-drawn Sesquicentennial Wagon Train was trudging along a winding 3,000-mile course from town to town (an event for which I had, in a moment of regretted weakness, agreed to help write and coproduce a film documentary), there were endless black-tie balls, rodeos, rattlesnake roundups, chili cookoffs, sheep shearings, outhouse races, air shows, and reenactments of all manner of historic events.

Organizers were even trotting out the state's literary crowd for proof that Texas did, in fact, have her own home-grown men and women of letters. It was all in good fun, and writers of everything from westerns to science fiction, romances to children's fables, were called to action. It was, we were told, our patriotic duty.

Which was my reason for being in Sherman, Texas, on the bright but chilly Saturday afternoon of March 22, 1986, for something called the Roundup of Texas Authors, an assembly of writers who had agreed to do readings, conduct workshops, autograph books, mingle, and sip fruit punch.

I was in the middle of an informal question-and-answer session with a roomful of aspiring young writers when a tall, grim-faced officer from the Sherman Police Department stuck his head inside the meeting room door and silently summoned me into the hallway.

"Are you Mister Stowers?"

I nodded.

"Sir," he said, "you need to call home immediately. It's an emergency." He politely refused to offer any additional information.

In the few frantic minutes it took me to locate a pay phone, myriad imagined tragedies played through my mind: a car accident; fire in a chimney I should have had cleaned; another heart attack suffered by my father.

A momentary rush of relief swept over me when after but a single ring I heard Pat's voice—strong, healthy, and safe. In a matter of seconds, however, all feeling of well-being was ripped away.

"Anson's in the hospital," she said, and I sensed anguish in her voice. She explained that she had received a call from the prison chaplain at Tennessee Colony informing her that my son was in a coma and had been rushed to the nearby Tyler Medical Center.

Immediately, she had telephoned the Sherman police and asked that they get word to me.

"The chaplain says you need to get there right away," Pat said. For a moment she waited for me to respond but I could offer only numbed silence.

"He's in critical condition," she finally added. "They don't know if he's going to make it. The chaplain said you had better hurry." Even in my confused state, I was aware that the message she'd been charged with passing along was difficult for her.

"What happened?"

"They said it was a drug overdose." The information she'd been given had been sketchy: Anson had been found lying unconscious on the floor of his cell. An attending nurse had at first thought he was dead, but after administering CPR was finally able to detect a faint pulse. Twice during the care flight trip to Tyler, prison medical personnel thought they had lost him. Pat suggested that I not detour through Dallas but instead drive directly to Tyler. "I'll meet you there," she said.

I replaced the receiver and stood for a moment in the silent auditorium hallway. Only then did I realize that the paper containing notes for my presentation had been wadded into a tight, moist ball during our brief conversation.

On legs suddenly weak and shaking, I walked into the parking lot, trying to focus my thoughts on the shortest route to Tyler.

I was already several miles down the interstate before it occurred to me that I had not bothered to explain my abrupt departure to anyone.

UNDER NORMAL CIRCUMSTANCES, a drive into the East Texas piney woods would be a pleasurable experience. Even before the dogwoods begin to bloom and the rolling countryside explodes in multiple shades of spring green, it is one of the most scenic regions of the state, dotted by small communities and lush farmland that evoke feelings of warm, peaceful nostalgia.

On this day, however, towns like Alba and Golden, Mineola and Lindale, where farmers in bib overalls drive slow-moving pickups to town for coffee shop conversation while their wives grocery shop at the A&P, were nothing more than a delaying nuisance. I sped along the shoreline of Lake Towakoni, all but unaware of its vast, quiet beauty.

As I drove, a single frightening thought hammered through my mind—one so fixed that I was unable to shake it despite concerted efforts: *My God, I'm going to have to make funeral arrangements for my own son.*

In a vain effort to brighten my thoughts, I attempted to call up memories of good times, those days before the angry rebellion and the drugs, courtrooms, and jails; the treasured times that every parent looks back on as touchstone moments: Little League games, birthday parties, Christmas mornings.

It was an exercise in futility for I was overwhelmed by the

dread and apprehension of the scene I was driving toward. A fear unlike any I'd ever experienced pounded in my chest, making the simple act of breathing a chore. I prayed to a God I was angry with for having allowed such a thing to happen. And as I neared the hospital the dread of what awaited wrapped around me like a dark and heavy cloud. I was vaguely aware of the moist warmth of tears on my face and quickly wiped them away and cursed. *You can't fall apart now.*

THE POLISHED TILE HALLWAY outside the Intensive Care Unit was tomblike quiet despite the presence of several families huddled in the nearby waiting area. An elderly couple held hands and stared blankly out the second-floor window, keeping vigil over some tragedy of their own. Across the way, a girl in her early teens silently studied the offerings of a soft drink machine. The only sound was the rapid squish made by the rubber-soled shoes of a nurse hurrying along the corridor.

As I pushed open the double doors leading to the ICU, ignoring a sign proclaiming that visitors were not welcome, it was unnecessary for anyone to direct me toward the small room where Anson was. Above the rhythmic beeps of monitors and whispered conversations near the nurses' station, I could hear an unfamiliar voice calling his name.

As I walked into the tiny room a nurse, her back to me, was leaning over the bed, shouting, "ANSON, YOU'VE GOT TO WAKE UP . . . OPEN YOUR EYES AND LOOK AT ME. TRY TO OPEN YOUR EYES . . . WAKE UP, ANSON . . ."

Standing in the doorway, I felt a sudden chill sweep through my body. A man standing at the opposite side of the bed, dressed in the khaki uniform of the Texas prison system, a holstered pistol on his hip, caught the nurse's eye and motioned in my direction.

She turned briefly, neither speaking nor smiling. Directing her attention back to the figure that I still could not see, she bent forward and began clapping her hands together, then resumed her shouting. "ANSON, LISTEN TO ME. YOUR FATHER'S HERE. WAKE UP AND TELL HIM HELLO . . ."

With that she motioned me toward the bed, stepping aside so that I could take her place. "He's pretty far under," she explained. "We've got to get him to fight it, to try to wake up."

I half stumbled to the bedside, getting my first glimpse of the pale, motionless form. Lying there, he looked so small, so fragile, almost childlike. His breathing, aided by a respirator, was shallow and slow. An IV bottle hung nearby, trailing a clear liquid into one arm. Oxygen tubes were attached to his nose.

"Talk to him," the nurse urged.

Bending forward, placing my face close to his ear, I called his name. "Hey, pal, it's me. I'm here."

"Louder," the nurse ordered.

We took turns yelling, pleading, trying to call him back from whatever dark hiding place he had retreated to.

WITH NIGHTFALL came a raging rainstorm. Streaks of lightning danced across the skies, frequently illuminating the room. Then, suddenly, a booming clap of thunder rattled the nearby window. Anson flinched at the sound, then I felt his hand tighten against mine.

A voice louder and more demanding than mine had managed to reach him.

For the next several hours I sat at his side, watching the tiny signs of progress. Several times his fingers moved ever so slightly. His eyelids would flutter briefly, as if he were trying to wake, but the task was obviously too difficult and the movement would soon stop. Occasionally he would make a faint, painful groan.

Still, for the first time since receiving Pat's call, I felt the return of optimism. Just moments later, when she entered the room, I was able to tell her with confidence that Anson was going to survive.

FOR THE REMAINDER of the night I sat near his bed, a montage of images playing through my mind. There, in that dimly lit room, I found myself thinking back on another trip to the hospital, one made long ago when the boys and I were living in the Texas Hill Country.

One spring afternoon, after the school bus had brought them home, Anson, then eleven, and Ashley, seven, had set off on an exploring trip into the nearby woods while I began to prepare dinner.

Later, as I sat at the kitchen table awaiting their return, I saw Anson emerge from a nearby cedar break, carrying his younger brother. Rushing to find out what had happened, I saw that both of their T-shirts were stained with blood from a long, jagged gash that had been torn in Ashley's arm. Both boys were in tears.

They had, Anson explained, been climbing over a fence when Ashley slipped and became tangled in the barbed wire.

We had rushed to the emergency room that day and waited anxiously as the doctor stitched the wound.

In the waiting room, I had purchased Anson a soft drink and sat with him, assuring him that his brother would be okay.

"How far did you carry him?" I asked.

"I dunno. A long way."

I hugged him tightly, prouder than I'd ever remembered being.

How, I wondered, could someone once so caring of others put such a small premium on his own life?

For a long time I stared down at him, my anxiety melting into an overwhelming sadness. Covering his arms were ugly, deep-purple tattoos that would, for the rest of his life, be a sign to the world that he was a convict.

How I abhorred the cruel, angry things he had done to himself. Almost as much as I did the fact that his wrist was handcuffed to the side of the bed.

I looked up to see that the prison guard was standing near the window, looking uncomfortable, almost apologetic. As if reading my mind, he glanced in the direction of the cuffs. "I'm sorry," he said, "but it's regulations."

I nodded but said nothing.

THE RAIN, which had greeted me upon my arrival, had returned, gently tapping a somber melody against the window of the tiny motel room I had checked into. In one corner the light of a muted television flickered, providing the only interruption to the late-night darkness.

Located just across the street from the hospital, the run-down facility's purpose clearly was convenience, not comfort. Few visitors, I was certain, bothered to complain about the musty smell of the rooms or the lack of a coffee shop or room service. It was, in truth, nothing more than a way station for the anxious.

After two days and nights in the ICU, watching as Anson

slowly regained consciousness, the nurses had clearly become weary of my constant presence and tired litany of questions and had, with only the slightest nod to diplomacy, suggested I seek more comfortable nighttime quarters.

Pat remained until the doctors assured us the crisis had passed, then placed a call to Anson's mother to inform her of the situation, and returned home. Before leaving she, too, had joined forces with the nurses, urging me to find a place that offered better sleeping accommodations than a hospital room chair.

Though I was physically and mentally drained, sleep came no easier in the motel bed than it had in the hospital. Finally, I had pulled a chair next to the window and sat, silently watching as the rain danced in the empty street outside.

An unshakable melancholy settled over me. The previous seventy-two hours has been consumed by the cold fear of death. Now, however, new emotions played through my mind. The relief that had come as Anson finally began to emerge from his coma had been replaced by an avalanche of soul-searching questions and an urgent demand for answers.

In the darkness of the motel room they spoke loudly to me.

Nothing in my experience had provided me any satisfactory explanation for one attempting to take his own life. The concept of suicide was as foreign to me as dead languages. I had not the slightest idea what depths of despair, pain, and self-disdain one might have to reach before losing the will to live. Yet in a room whose lighted window I could see from my solitary vantage point, my son lay fighting to survive just such a decision.

Why? What had driven him to such an act?

Once alert, Anson firmly insisted that suicide had never been his intent. His cell mate, he explained, had been suffering from a lengthy bout with severe anxiety, and regular doses of an antidepressant called Sinequan had been prescribed for him. The inmate had described to Anson how "mellow" the medication made him feel and had given him two of the pills.

The resulting coma, Anson insisted, had been the by-product of nothing more than a bad reaction to his experimentation with the Sinequan.

How I wanted to believe him, to embrace the relief that my son had not wished to kill himself. Yet when I posed Anson's scenario to one of the attending doctors his reply was a noncommital shrug that spoke volumes. He'd seen too many suicide attempts not to recognize the symptoms.

We spoke no more of it. Once back in prison, I had been assured, Anson would be watched closely and undergo a thorough psychiatric evaluation. For the time being, I determined to focus on the fact that the immediate crisis had passed.

His spirits, meanwhile, rose greatly when I told him that Pat was putting Annette on the bus and that I would pick her up early in the evening and bring her to the hospital. The prospect of seeing his wife prompted a sudden renewal of energy and returned a faint but evident sparkle to his eyes. In anticipation of her visit he asked me to purchase him a comb, shaving gear, toothpaste, and a toothbrush.

One of the nurses volunteered to give him a haircut.

WITH ANNETTE'S ARRIVAL, my presence was no longer necessary. After the doctor determined that Anson would fully recover and had him moved from the Intensive Care Unit, the prison guard agreed to allow her to stay with him.

I said my good-byes, had Anson promise to call me with

reports of his recuperation, and turned my thoughts to the trip home.

As I neared the door, Anson called out and motioned me back to his bed. Extending his hand, he looked up at me silently for several seconds, then spoke in a whisper. "I'm going to be okay," he said.

THERE IS A UNIQUE FRUSTRATION attached to dealing with things beyond one's control. While I still felt a strong sense of responsibility for Anson, a need to try and point him toward a more positive and productive course, the truth of the matter was I had very little input into his daily life. That task had been assumed by authorities of the Texas prison system. They told him when to wake and sleep, when to eat, what to wear, where to be, and what he could and couldn't do.

Years earlier, I was assigned a magazine piece on a Texas prison inmate named O'Neal Browning who had, as a youngster, received a life sentence for the ax murder of his father. During his incarceration, Browning had gained celebrity status as one of the star performers in the Huntsville Prison Rodeo, once an annual event that drew thousands of spectators. By the time I met him he had been named the event's All-Round Cowboy seven times, which was a record. Browning delighted in the recognition. The rodeo had become the focus of his life. In prison he had become somebody.

At one point, in fact, he had been paroled and settled in Dallas where he worked at odd jobs—driving a truck, doing landscaping, breaking horses for a local rancher—while trying to adjust to life on the outside.

But as the October date for the rodeo grew nearer, Browning's thoughts turned to past glories. To assure himself a shot at yet another championship he robbed a liquor store, then promptly turned himself in.

The system, clearly, had become more comfortable for O'Neal Browning than life in the real world. I did not want that to become the case with my son.

Anson, still rebellious and determined to set his own rules of behavior, remained at odds with both worlds. The underlying tone of his brief letters was always that of angry frustration: *"I'm really getting tired of this crap . . ."* or *". . . nothing new on this end, just another boring week."*

Compounding his problems was the fact that correspondence from Annette had dwindled to only an occasional note—a complaint I came to expect in each letter I received. Following his release from the hospital and return to Tennessee Colony, I had volunteered to drive Annette to the prison for weekend visitation any time she wished to go. After only a couple of trips, however, she showed little interest. And despite Anson's repeated requests that I urge her to come see him, I didn't press the matter.

Neither did I mention to him that Annette had confided to me that she was contemplating divorce.

Their marriage, I was certain, was fast coming to an end. And while I had encouraged her to focus her priorities on her own well-being and get on with her life, I harbored a deep concern over how Anson would deal with the fact that she would not be waiting when he was finally released.

IN TRUTH, I found myself dreading the day the parole board would again set my son free. For all of Anson's insistences that lessons had been learned and the error of his ways finally realized, my hope simply would not translate into real optimism. The scales were weighted so heavily against him. How does a high school dropout with a lengthy list of felony arrests find his way back into society? What employer is willing to risk the offer of a worthwhile job to a heavily tattooed ex-con with an unimpressive work history and a record of drug abuse? Where does one so violently opposed to the rules that govern the go-along-to-get-along world fit in?

They were questions I allowed to visit only occasionally as I chose to follow the same advice I had offered to Annette. It was time to get on with my own life.

Anson's troubles aside, things had never been better. Any reservations I might have had about remarrying had long been put aside. Pat, loving and supportive, brought a brightness to each new day, and I worked toward the completion of *Careless Whispers* with a confidence I'd never before experienced.

IT IS NONSENSE, I know, but throughout my adult life I have entertained a nagging distrust of good fortune. There is a paranoid voice deep inside that warns of some omnipotent balancing scale ever ready to make certain that equal amounts of good fortune and bad rule my life. It is, I know, a ridiculously flawed attitude, a belief with no sane, logical foundation that has routinely made me wary of those feelings of personal well-being or professional success. Subconsciously, I have always greeted good news with a tangible dread that bad must soon follow. For reasons I neither like nor understand, I spend an undue amount of time waiting for the other shoe to drop.

In the wake of its publication, *Careless Whispers* enjoyed warm reviews and brisk sales. It rose steadily on the local best-seller lists, which were printed weekly in the Dallas papers, and there was talk of Hollywood interest. Then came word from New York that it had been selected as one of five finalists for the prestigious Edgar Allan Poe Award, which is given annually by the Mystery Writers of America to the year's best fact crime book. More important, the people about whom I had written and felt such a strong bond with during my research had, to my relief, embraced the book.

One late January Saturday afternoon in 1987, as Pat and I were attending an autograph party at a mall bookstore, two women I was acquainted with, mother and aunt of one of the victims I'd written about, stopped by for a surprise visit. We chatted briefly, then Pat went off to have lunch with them while I was left the uncomfortable task of sitting behind a stack of books, trying to strike a nonchalant pose that would convince shoppers I was not a beggar on display.

Later, as we drove toward home, Pat mentioned that one of the women she'd lunched with had confided that she had recently undergone surgery for the removal of several small breast tumors. Fortunately, a biopsy had shown them to be benign and all was well.

That said, Pat fell quiet for the remainder of the trip then quickly disappeared into the bathroom immediately upon our arrival home. Only a few minutes passed before she emerged, pale and frightened.

"I've found a lump," she said.

My initial reaction was the hope that her "discovery" was nothing more than the result of a powerful and frightening suggestion planted in her mind earlier in the day. I knew, however, that Pat was not given to hysterics or overreaction. If she thought she felt a lump in her breast, there was good reason to believe one was there.

The remainder of the weekend crept by slowly. It would be Monday—suddenly an eternity away—before she could see her doctor, and little I said or did offered relief from the sudden terror that had invaded our lives. A suffocating gloom set in to accompany the seemingly endless wait.

In a matter of days, however, her worst suspicions had been confirmed. The tumor in her right breast was not only real but also malignant. Lymph nodes had also been infected by the deadly disease. A mastectomy was scheduled for the second week in February.

There is no proper way to define the overwhelming sense of helplessness one experiences as he watches a loved one endure the tortures associated with cancer. No words or actions can deflect the stark fear that accompanies the sudden, terrifying confrontation with mortality. Though strong-willed, Pat was consumed by the knowledge that the doctor's diagnosis offered the very real possibility that she might soon die. No recitation of statistics offering proof that a high percentage of women suffering from her type of cancer survive provided any real comfort. Determined and optimistic one minute, she would be overwhelmed by a paralyzing fear the next. There was nothing in the disease's ugly history that could provide the guarantee she so badly wished for.

The affliction I dealt with was frustration. I repeatedly offered hollow promises that all would soon be well, that our life would return to normal once the surgery was completed. I searched constantly for diversions—movies, ball games, long walks—anything that might, however briefly, take Pat's mind off the agony that had beset her. At best, they were but stopgap measures.

All attempts at regaining some sense of normalcy failed miserably. I continued to work on a new book but without any real passion or sense of urgency. For the first time in years, the problems of my son were pushed far out of my mind. It was as if the outside world had suddenly ceased to exist.

The surgery, performed on a cold, lead sky day, brought a new flood of unexpected emotions. In its immediate aftermath there was a feeling best described as euphoria. The cancerous tumor had been removed; a welcomed distancing from the dreaded disease had been achieved. Even in her frail and weakened postoperative condition, Pat's face radiated relief.

The hard part, I tried to assure her, was over. In truth, it was just beginning.

The operation, doctors told us, had been successful. And while they could offer no absolute guarantee that the cancer might not one day recur, the prognosis was good. The critical time frame, they told us, would be five years. If the cancer did not recur during that time, odds were excellent that it never would.

What remained, then, was a series of chemotherapy treatments, taken at three-week intervals, that would be agonizing. Not only did each session make her violently ill for a twelve-hour period immediately afterward, but they also robbed her of all energy. Getting up to read the morning paper and sip a cup of tea was a draining ordeal that quickly forced her back to bed. The antinausea medication's only effect was to erase her memory for several days following each application. All food lost its taste. A suddenly elusive attention span, created by the medication, made attempts at reading a frustrating exercise.

Adding to her angst was the fact that she had begun to lose her hair.

But as spring approached she insisted that we make plans to travel to New York and attend the Edgar Awards banquet. "You're going to win," she repeatedly insisted, "and I want to be there to see it."

With that she shopped for a prosthesis and a wig while I made travel arrangements.

Though Pat had never before visited New York, she acknowledged with little argument that the traditions of sightseeing and sampling Big Apple entertainment would have to wait until another time. Her small measure of energy, she said, would be saved for the awards banquet.

Thus we arrived in the early afternoon of the day of the ceremonies and took a cab directly to the hotel. The trip had been exhausting, and Pat went immediately to bed. Not wishing to disturb her rest and feeling the first twinges of anxiety over the announcement that would be made but a few hours later, I wandered the streets of Manhattan.

Long before I made my way back to our room I had become convinced that the trip was pure folly. The track records of the other four finalists had far outdistanced *Careless Whispers*. Two of the nominated books—Alan Prendergast's *The Poison Tree* and *Incident at Big Sky* by Johnny France and Malcolm McConnell—had already been made into highly applauded made-for-television movies, and another, Nicholas Pileggi's *Wiseguy,* had spent several months on the *New York Times* best-seller list and was being scripted for the big screen. The other, *Unveiling Claudia,* was authored by award-winning novelist and university professor Daniel Keyes, a writer whose talents I greatly admired.

Yet that evening in the Sheraton Centre's main ballroom Pat became a prophet. *Careless Whispers* was announced as the winner of the Edgar.

On the morning following the awards ceremony, I awoke abruptly at first light, my initial thought that the entire experience had been nothing more than some fickle dream. Sitting up in bed, I squinted across the room to make certain the porcelain statuette of the legendary poet-novelist was, in fact, on the bureau where I'd left it.

Relieved, I quietly dressed and slipped out, leaving Pat to sleep until a more reasonable hour.

During those gray dawning hours the city of New York is quiet, catnapping after a long night's activity and not quite ready to awake and begin the new day. I encountered few pedestrians as I walked along Seventh Avenue, stopping for a *New York Times* at a corner newsstand, then a styrofoam cup of coffee.

I found my way to Central Park and took my pick of the deserted benches. There I sat reading the paper, interrupted only by the begging of pigeons and the occasional passing of an early-morning jogger.

I had been there perhaps a half hour when a sudden, unexplainable feeling of utter despair swept over me—a dark, oppressive visitor smothering what should have been the happiest moment of my professional life.

Instead of savoring the recognition my book had received just hours earlier, I found myself thinking of Pat, sick and sleeping restlessly in a nearby hotel room, and of Anson, in a faraway prison, his life not affected in the least by my moment of good fortune.\

The copper-bright early morning now ambushed by inner storm clouds, I slowly rose to return to the hotel. The joyous feeling of having won something was overwhelmed by a cold, unpalatable fear of losing everything.

Nine

TIME IS, INDEED, NATURE'S greatest healer. Having made her way through the chemotherapy treatments, Pat underwent reconstructive surgery and slowly began to regain her strength. Her hair grew back, hints of renewed energy and confidence finally became evident, and her sleep was interrupted less often by fears that the dreaded cancer might recur.

A fragile, welcomed optimism was returning.

Work began to go well on the new book, the story of a young

undercover narcotics officer who had been placed in a rural Texas high school, posing as a senior. After only two months, twenty-one-year-old George Raffield's real identity had become suspected, and he was lured to an isolated pasture near Midlothian, Texas, where he expected to be introduced to a drug dealer. Instead, he was shot and killed by a sixteen-year-old sophomore, the son of a Dallas police officer.

In the book I hoped to examine the effects of the crime on a small, bucolic community where, years earlier, Anson had experienced his first serious encounter with law enforcement after wrecking a stolen car. My intent was to focus not so much on the murder but instead on the scars it had left on the residents. I planned to title it *Innocence Lost*.

Because of Pat's illness and the research demands of a new writing deadline, my prison visits with Anson had become increasingly irregular. Still, we stayed in touch by letter and telephone.

Anson, meanwhile, was having troubles of his own—things with which I could offer no real help.

In the spring of 1988 Annette finally filed for a divorce, and immediately the tone of Anson's letters became a mixture of renewed anger and self-pity, filled with confused ramblings. If there was any genuine enthusiasm for a future that awaited him in the outside world, I failed to detect it.

In fact, as his parole date neared, I began to anticipate his release with growing dread. Though he was twenty-five years old, I still viewed him as a deeply troubled child with no real sense of the basic survival requirements demanded of adult society. Which all gave rise to a new dilemma.

Though we had not discussed it, I knew that Anson fully

expected to be welcomed again into our home, returning to the old bedroom he'd settled into following his previous release. As before, we would be expected to help him find transportation and a job, and assist with the myriad small details required to get reestablished in the outside world: renewal of driver's license, buying new clothes, and setting up visits with yet another new parole officer. In a sense, the transition from prison inmate to parolee is not unlike that of an alien visitor attempting to gain citizenship, battling bureaucratic red tape on one hand and public indifference on the other.

Society offers no welcome mat for the ex-con. And, though it troubled me greatly to admit it, neither could I this time around.

The tension and unease that had permeated our home following his previous release was not something I could allow to recur. In all good conscience I simply could not put Pat through such anxieties again and would take no chance that her recovery might be hampered in any way by stress created by Anson's presence. Nor, in truth, did I wish to deal once more with the day-to-day arguments that his immediate presence promised. It was, I reasoned, long past time for my son to make a life of his own—on his own.

Pat had reluctantly admitted her concerns—"I just don't know if I can deal with it again," she had said—and was visibly relieved when I told her that Anson would not be returning to our home.

How she might have reacted had I lobbied to give it one more try, I honestly don't know. She had long been supportive of my attempts on Anson's behalf and, better than anyone, knew the private agonies I felt at the continual failures. At the same time, her attitude toward our life together had undergone a subtle but certain change in the wake of her bout with cancer. Forced to consider her own mortality for the first time, she had repeatedly expressed her determination to focus on the positive, to make every effort to assure the quality of those days, months, and years remaining to us.

And while I had refused even to consider the possibility that our time might be cut short by a recurrence of her illness, it was a philosophy I embraced heartily. My wife's well-being and the life we shared was, above all, something I was determined to protect.

Still, it did not make the decision easy.

Perhaps, I reasoned, Anson might actually benefit from a more gradual reentry into society, first moving into a halfway house where a three-month period of counseling and participation in drug-awareness programs was mandatory. With a better understanding of the potential hazards that a parolee is certain to face, his chances of making a new start might well improve. And I hoped it would remove some of his dependency on me and allow him time to search out career and educational options available to him.

At the Dallas County Residential Facility, parolees use the ninety days to find a job, save some money, take advantage of programs like Alcoholics and Drugs Anonymous, and find a permanent residence. Though the routine is severely structured and rules are strictly enforced, residents are free to come and go in search of work, receive visitors, and earn weekend furloughs.

In theory it may have sounded good, a plan based on logic and sound principle. In truth, however, I had long been convinced that the halfway house release program was a shameful waste of taxpayer time and money. I chose not to admit my great sense of doubt to Pat.

Only months earlier I had spent a considerable amount of time visiting the halfway house where Anson would likely be sent upon his release and had written a lengthy and rather disturbing magazine piece on what takes place inside the old two-story red brick building located in a rundown area of Dallas. The sixty men in residence at the time of my research ran the gamut from murderers to sex offenders, armed robbers to drug dealers. Some had been in the Texas prison system as many as three times before the Board of Pardons and Paroles had sent them to the half-way house.

I interviewed numerous parolees who spoke freely of the quick availability of drugs and alcohol within walking distance, saw men in a chemically induced stupor sitting hour after hour in a dayroom, blankly staring at a television until time for their next meal or another mind-numbing injection of psychotropics like Thorazine, Haldol, or Prolixin, administered by one of the staff members. Two of the residents immodestly confided that they had robbed a convenience store just days earlier. And there was still talk of a homicide committed by a resident the previous March. Mentally disturbed and on medication, this man had left the facility and brutally murdered a prominent Dallas civil rights lawyer and his wife. Police had found the couple lying in their bed and counted no less than 120 stab wounds on their bodies. The motive: He'd liked the suits he'd seen the attorney wearing and had wanted them for himself.

I sat in the office of administrator Beverly Daberko one afternoon as she took a call from a mental hospital in Wichita Falls and listened as she angrily refused to accept transfer of an inmate who, just days earlier, had attempted to take his own life by setting himself on fire. Previously he'd attempted suicide by drinking a large amount of ammonia. "We're expected to perform miracles here," she had wearily told me.

The halfway house had become, in truth, little more than an extension of the prison system. "We provide the beds that TDC no longer has," she admitted.

And this was the environment into which I was, in a manner of speaking, going to send my son—a jail without locks on the doors but a jail just the same. Weighing the choices available to me, I had opted to send him into a situation where, statistics showed, 20 percent return to prison before their ninety-day transition period is completed.

Anson's reaction was predictable.

I had written him a lengthy letter in which I tried to explain my thoughts about his upcoming parole, assured him that I still stood ready to help him begin his new life, and urged him to give the halfway house a chance.

In response I received a terse note: "Thanks for allowing me the opportunity to exit through the asshole of TDC," Anson wrote. He went on to remind me of negative observations I'd made to him following my research into the Dallas facility. What I had done, he insisted, was "kick him squarely in the gut."

It was a ploy that had become all too common over the years: my son heaping all blame for his problems onto my shoulders. And as if reacting on cue, my first feelings were those of doubt and guilt. This time, however, they were not lingering. What, I found myself asking, gave him the right to again throw my life into turmoil? Where was the fairness in my playing the role of problem solver only to be chastized for shortcomings he quickly perceived when things failed to meet his approval? I had suddenly grown bone weary of the one-sidedness and was angry at Anson for his behavior and myself for allowing it to affect me so negatively. I found that the anger felt good.

His letter was the last time I would hear from him for months.

He did not, in fact, even bother to inform me of his release date.

On the afternoon of August 29, 1988, Anson arrived at the Greyhound Bus Station in downtown Dallas with instructions to contact his parole officer and report to the halfway house within twenty-four hours or risk arrest and return to prison. In his pocket was what was left of the "gate money" he'd received upon his release from TDC.

By legislative decree, every parolee is given civilian clothing and $200 in cash on the day he is set free. As he'd done in the past, Anson went directly to a discount clothing store near the bus station and purchased jeans and a T-shirt to replace the ill-fitting prison-issued slacks and sports shirt. A pair of cowboy boots brought his bill to $65. By the time he'd purchased a $35 bus ticket, his bankroll had been reduced by half.

Actually, he'd done better than do many released prisoners. Stories of parolees spending every cent within a few hours of their release are not uncommon. Clothes, an extravagant meal, and an hour or so with a local prostitute eager to reacquaint an ex-con with sexual pleasures can drain away a couple of hundred dollars quickly.

One of the favored and oft-told stories passed among prison officials concerns an ex-con whose spending spree left him broke within an hour of his release. When it suddenly dawned on him that he had no way to get home he opted to hot-wire a pickup parked in downtown Huntsville. He had not even made it to the city limits in the stolen truck before he was pulled over, arrested, and taken to jail where he was charged with auto theft. His long-awaited freedom had lasted barely two hours.

Enjoying the sweet taste of freedom for the first time in three years, Anson did nothing so drastic. Still, as he arrived in Dallas, he clearly had no intention of abiding by the rules. Getting a ride with friends of a fellow bus passenger, he had gone directly to the club where Annette worked, purchased a vial of the crystallized methamphetamine known as crank, and convinced her to check into a motel with him. Within three hours of his return he was high.

In the days that followed he outlined for her an ill-conceived plan he had formulated in the days prior to his release. Rather than deal with the demands and authority of halfway house staff members and the constant prying of a parole officer, he would simply disappear into Mexico and there begin a new life for himself. He'd had all he could stand of people watching over him, offering unsolicited advice, telling him what he could and couldn't do.

The idea had the ring of a wistfully planned adolescent adventure, and Annette was finally successful in convincing him it was a bad idea. She urged Anson to give the halfway house a chance—after all, it was only for ninety days—before running away to what would be almost certainly new legal problems.

A week late, he finally reported to his parole officer and moved into the halfway house. If there was concern over his tardy arrival, no one bothered to express it. The truth of the matter was that the overburdened system had neither time nor manpower to concern itself with the absence of one lost soul.

Still, it took only two weeks for Anson to run afoul of the rules. One evening, after a visit from Annette, they had walked to her car, which was parked several blocks away. Though he'd been gone for less than thirty minutes, Anson was later told that because he had left the building after curfew, his weekend pass privileges would be revoked.

It was all the excuse he needed. In a burst of temper he packed his belongings and immediately left. The following day he phoned his parole officer and lied, saying he had been "thrown out."

The parole officer's only response was to ask if Anson had a place to stay.

"I'm going to move in with my wife," Anson replied.

A few days later the parole official stopped by the apartment, visited briefly with Anson and Annette, and routinely approved the new living arrangement.

I knew none of this at the time. I was, in fact, resigned to the knowledge that I would not hear from Anson until some crisis developed that demanded my involvement. His anger toward me would prohibit anything shy of a call for help. And that, I reasoned, would come only as a last resort.

Any contact, Anson knew, was almost certain to open the door to resented questions about his well-being and future plans and advice he was not in the least interested to hear. We had, in a manner of speaking, reached a communication impasse: He did not want me prying into anything about his life. I, on the other hand, wanted desperately to know how he was doing but vowed to maintain the space between us and made no attempt to contact him.

Then late one evening, several weeks following his parole, he finally called. He spoke briefly of his original plan to flee into Mexico, crediting Annette with convincing him to stay with her. They were "back together," he said, and things were going well.

He had gotten a job at an automobile paint shop on Harry Hines Boulevard.

I listened and waited to learn the real purpose of the call.

Finally, it came: Annette had fallen behind on her car payments and it had been repossessed. Could I loan them the money to get her car back?

Despite my growing resentment at being viewed as little more than a convenient, quick-service bank, I agreed to the loan, fully aware that what I was once again doing was making an irrational and probably ill-advised attempt to what? Buy my way back into my son's life?

Anson gave me directions to the paint shop, and we scheduled a time to meet the following morning.

IN THOSE TIMES of quiet desperation that Thoreau warned us of from his Walden Pond cabin long ago, man's perceptions often become dramatically blurred. We allow our mind's eye to play convenient tricks; we see what we want to see or else we see nothing at all. Hopes are miraculously transformed into false realities that lend the briefest moments of calming, welcomed comfort.

Wearing a khaki jumpsuit, Anson was sweeping out one of the automotive bays when I arrived. He looked tired and thin, but the pasty complexion of prison life had been replaced by a healthy tan and his hair was now longer and neatly parted. He was in the early stages of growing a mustache.

He greeted me with a smile and a firm handshake and we chatted briefly, neither really comfortable in the other's presence. Anson talked about his job, gave me a quick tour of the building, and introduced me to his boss. In less than fifteen minutes we had exhausted our attempts at small talk, and I had given him the money and was on my way back to the parking lot.

"Look," Anson said as I got into my car, "I appreciate your helping us out like this. As soon as I get on my feet a little better I'll pay you back."

I knew full well he never would.

He promised to stay in touch, then turned away. "I'd better get back to work."

The brief scene had, at best, been awkward. Yet not at all unfamiliar. I'd long since lost track of the times in recent years when I had walked away from my son with the feeling that there was so much left unsaid; issues too long ignored literally cried out for resolutions that would never come. But how, in God's name, was that to be accomplished when neither of us seemed capable any longer of grasping the simple rules of honesty and trust that provided the foundation for meaningful dialogue? Our conversations had become little more than hollow noise that filled anxious moments until we could both go our separate ways.

All that aside, I was relieved to see that he had found a job and displayed enthusiasm for the work. As I drove away I felt faintly optimistic about my son for the first time in a while.

What I had seen was an illusion, and my positive feelings were again fueled by a gullible willingness to view things not as they were but as they seemed.

H I S " J O B " at the paint shop never existed. The manager, a friend of Anson's, had agreed to tell anyone who asked that my son was an employee. On those days when his parole officer was scheduled to stop by and make mandatory checks on his progress,

Anson would, in fact, be there, going through the motions of work.

The same ruse also worked effectively on me. Occasionally I would phone only to be told that Anson was "out on a delivery." His "boss" would assure me that he'd have him call as soon as he returned, then would contact Anson to alert him that I had called. Without fail, he would be in touch sometime later in the day, inventing elaborate details of how busy he'd been.

In truth, he had begun making deliveries for a local drug dealer.

In the weeks following his release, I saw my son only that one time, yet he was regularly in my thoughts. At the most unusual moments, sometimes while in the midst of working, mowing the yard, or even reading a book or watching television in the evenings, I would be suddenly overwhelmed by anxiety and find myself wishing to know where he was and if he was all right. It would come quickly, rarely prompted by conversation or any other logical provocation, and would often weigh on me for hours.

And there were the dreams. In them I would see him at a distance, generally in some crowded place, and I would attempt to get his attention. Always without success.

Since so much of my work had begun to focus on the psychology of criminal behavior, I found it impossible not to occasionally compare the personality traits of those about whom I was writing and those of my own son. It was a disturbing exercise that had begun to visit my consciousness all too regularly. I had listened as criminals reflected on ruined lives that had begun with minor transgressions and gradually eroded into full-fledged lawless behavior that resulted in their imprisonment. Helpful psychologists and psychiatrists had patiently shared their insights, offering clinical explanations. I'd heard blame placed on impoverished backgrounds, myriad social injustices, and the many forms of early parental abuse. Veteran police officers and prosecutors, many hopelessly jaded by years of experience, were often quick to lump all lawbreakers into a single category: bad people without the slightest trace of virtue.

Still, either because I was not willing to look closely enough or because I simply refused to acknowledge truths that were obvious, I could not, for the life of me, see the kinship between my son and those criminal strangers I had encountered and written about.

My son was not like them. He couldn't possibly be. Still, I had to wonder why his life had taken such a disastrous course.

Years later he would confide to me that each move during my toils as a newspaperman had been an agonizing experience. "I never had a lot of what I considered really close friends," he said, "and when I had to leave those I did like behind it really upset me. Finally, I just said 'to hell with it' and quit trying to make new ones because I figured the time would come when we'd move again. So I decided to keep to myself as much as I could."

With the exception of those years spent in the idyllic, pressure-free countryside near Comfort, he could not remember any real adolescent happiness. Which, in retrospect, I find interesting in light of my own observation that the community, its mores, and its attitudes had seemed far more reflective of the long-past fifties, when I'd come of age.

Anson's later attempts at athletics, he told me, had been futile attempts to please me. "I had little interest in sports and certainly no real ability. I never remember you actually pushing me to come out for the football team or to play baseball, but so much of your life revolved around sports that the message was pretty clear. I knew it would please you if I showed some interest. So, I faked it. If nothing else, by giving it a try I proved to you that I wasn't ever going to be worth a shit as an athlete."

Drugs, he admitted, eventually became his escape from personal failures and unfulfilled expectations. "The only time my problems went away, the only time I felt good, was when I was high," he said.

IT WAS THE FIRST WEEK in November when Anson called with another request. When he'd been sent to prison, I had stored his clothing and personal items in boxes and put them away in the attic. On several occasions since his release I had asked if he wanted them, and his reply had always been the same: He'd get around to picking them up when he had time.

Now, however, there was a sudden urgency.

"Can you bring them this afternoon?" he asked.

"Sure. What's going on?"

"Listen, Dad, you really don't want to know."

"Yes, I do."

"Just think back to my original plan, okay? That's all I'm going to say." He then gave me directions to a billiards parlor in north Dallas where he would meet me at 4 P.M.

Why this clandestine meeting? Wouldn't it be simpler for me just to take them to where he and Annette were living? Or drop them off where he was working? What prevented him from coming to the house and picking them up himself? Once again the familiar gut feeling that something bad was about to happen swept over me.

"Are you in some kind of trouble?"

He insisted he wasn't, yet there was an agitated tone to his voice that begged difference.

For some time after hanging up the phone I sat wondering what new turn of events had taken place in my lost son's life. I detailed the brief conversation to Pat, pointing out that he'd made it clear he did not want me visiting where he lived or knowing what his plans were.

"What's this all about?" Pat asked, clearly agitated by the position in which Anson was again placing me.

"I think he's going to run. Probably to Mexico."

"Why?"

"I don't have the slightest idea."

A look of anger gradually spread across my wife's face as she shook her head. For the first time she lashed out against Anson, bitter private resentments finally bursting into the open. "Why does he keep doing this to you?" she asked. "God, how I hate it. When's enough? Why can't he just go away and give you some peace?"

With that she rose and hurried from my office, surprised, I think, at her own sudden outburst. A few minutes later she had found a large suitcase and was silently packing Anson's things.

In the haste of our conversation he had given me the wrong directions. Instead of a billiards parlor, there was a convenience store at the intersection I'd driven to. I pulled into the parking lot and waited for almost two hours.

A discomforting feeling accompanied my wait. If, in fact, Anson was planning to escape from some kind of new legal problem, was there a possibility that my involvement might be viewed as an illegal act? I was, after all, aware that the rules of his parole forbade his leaving Dallas County without permission. To do so could result in his return to prison. And while he'd been careful not to explain fully to me the sudden need for the clothing, precious little guesswork was necessary to determine what he was planning. Again, I felt drawn very near to an unlawful act and was experiencing an overwhelming sense of frustration that was again building toward outright anger.

Weary of waiting, I phoned Pat shortly after six to explain that Anson had not arrived and to ask if he had called. He hadn't. "Just come on home," she urged.

Later that evening we finally connected. Calling again, Anson said that he'd realized too late that he'd given me the wrong street address. "I'm sorry I put you to so much trouble," he apologized. Still, he needed the clothing right away. "Could you bring them to the apartment complex?"

"Anson," I said, "I'm really tired of this shit. Let's get it over with. Just tell me how to get there."

With that he gave me directions to where he and Annette were living. "There's a big Timberline Apartments sign on the corner," he said. "I'll meet you there."

I told him I would be there in an hour.

HE WAS WEARING JEANS and a dark T-shirt, leaning against the sign marking the entrance to a maze of apartment dwellings. Nearby, smoke from a barbecue grill floated from a balcony porch into the last remnants of daylight, and laughing voices from a coed softball game echoed across the well-manicured lawn. It was a much nicer place than I'd expected.

Pulling to the curb, I unloaded the heavy suitcase without comment as Anson approached. I had vowed en route to ask no questions and remain no longer than necessary.

We stood there, like strangers in the late fall twilight, looking at each other for several seconds without speaking. It was Anson who finally broke the silence. "Dad, I appreciate you doing this."

There was an unforgivable awkwardness to the moment, and I found myself wanting to be gone as quickly as possible. What was there to say? One more wasted plea that he turn from the self-wounding course he seemed so determined to travel? Did I say good-bye and wish him well on whatever absurd journey he had in mind?

The mood was briefly lightened when Annette walked up, smiling as she tucked her arm into Anson's, and said hello. I hadn't seen her in months, not since our last trip together to the prison visiting room, and she appeared well and happy.

"You having any luck keeping this guy in line?" I asked her, making sure she recognized my words were a jest rather than a probing question. She smiled and rolled her eyes in a mocking answer. "Sometimes," she replied.

It was a good exit line. They turned after saying good-bye and began walking back toward the apartments.

I felt a wave of sadness as I stood, leaning against the hood of the car for a moment, watching as Anson struggled with the weight of the suitcase until they disappeared into the fast-lengthening shadows cast by the buildings.

On the drive home I had no way of knowing that I would never see Annette again. Or that it would be the last time I'd see my son as a free man.

Ten

WHETHER THE IDEA OF becoming a drug dealer had struck Anson after his release from prison, coming as some spur-of-the-moment brainstorm like so many of his ideas, or was something he'd been planning a long time, I didn't know.

Only much later was I able to piece together the sequence of events that set the course. Among the prison companions he'd spent a good deal of time with had been an inmate who was serving a sentence for operating a methamphetamine lab. He had detailed for Anson the lucrative nature of the business, pointing out that the start-up cost, including necessary glassware and chemicals, was only about $5,000. In turn, a single "cook" could result in a profit of $75,000 to $100,000. The inmate shared with him the recipe for preparing illegal drugs with street names like "speed," "crank," "go-fast," and "crystal."

That the inmate's enterprise had ended in arrest and imprisonment was obviously not viewed as a warning by Anson.

The only problem he recognized was that of somehow amassing the necessary capital to get into the business. Subsequently, a fellow resident at the halfway house suggested he enter the drug trade as a courier. As a "mule" or "runner," he could not only learn the business from an inside vantage point and make valuable contacts, but could also accumulate the desired bankroll in a relatively short time if he saved his earnings.

"That," his advisor reminded, "means staying away from the shit yourself."

It was not something Anson was able to do.

Usually paid in small amounts of the drugs he was delivering—amphetamines that he, in turn, could sell—he had immediately fallen into a routine of getting high on his "profits."

Quickly his plans disappeared into a constant drug-induced haze. He slept rarely and ate little. When not on the streets plying his newfound trade, he sat for hours in the darkened apartment, watching television or nervously pacing the floor. Overwhelming paranoia, one of the chief side effects of amphetamine abuse, became his constant companion, and his mood turned darker and more angry with each passing day. The slightest provocation moved him to outrageous behavior. One evening, in a sudden fit of rage triggered by some passing remark an apartment tenant had made to Annette, Anson picked up a baseball bat and chased the man for several blocks, screaming curses and threats before finally calming and abandoning the pursuit. Feeling the need for protection, he purchased a .357 Magnum from a neighbor who had once worked as a security guard.

Meanwhile, he and Annette began to argue constantly about his drug usage, their confrontations becoming more physical than ever. Trapped in Anson's downward spiral, she demanded that he leave on numerous occasions, but each time he refused. Though no longer married, Annette had become the typical, tragic example of the battered, abused wife unable to find her way out of what had become an ongoing nightmare.

IN LATE OCTOBER of 1988, Anson had met a man named Don Wiley, a sharp dresser in his mid-to-late thirties who had begun frequenting the club where Annette was working. In short order a friendship developed. They would sit in the club for hours, talking cars and music, paying little attention to the stage where an endless procession of topless women, Annette among them, performed to the blaring music.

In time Wiley confided that he was in the market for amphetamines to provide to some of the customers of a thriving automobile repair business he owned. And when Anson suggested he might be able to help him out, Wiley casually expressed interest in learning more about the big money that he'd heard the drug trade promised.

The kinship was struck. Anson, impressed by his newfound friend's talk of business successes, was soon detailing his plan to set up his own meth lab, a venture that required only modest funding that he had yet to put together. The plan obviously interested Wiley, who was soon asking more and more questions about the potential earnings of such an operation, how long it would take to see a profit, and what level of legal risk might be involved. Anson had quick, assuring answers for every question.

Wiley then began talking of a possible partnership, providing the start-up money for the operation. In turn, Anson would agree to supply him with five to ten pounds of amphetamines per month. By evening's end they had a deal.

In the meantime, however, Wiley needed to make a buy immediately to satisfy the needs of his business associates. Anson, riding a new kind of high, agreed to introduce him to the person for whom he'd been working.

A WOMAN in her early thirties named Janis Latham was the person Anson's halfway house friend had suggested he contact if he was interested in getting into the business. Upon meeting her, Anson's initial impression was that her appearance did little to suggest a successful drug dealer. Overweight and unkempt, she wore jeans and a man's dress shirt, disdained makeup, and wore her long yellow-blond hair in a ponytail. She, her live-in boyfriend, and two other men had joined forces and grown into moderately successful drug suppliers in a short time.

Before Anson expressed a willingness to deliver the drugs they were manufacturing, the task had often fallen to Janis's fourteen-year-old son. "It was the safest way," she explained, "because a juvenile isn't going to serve any prison time if he does get arrested."

She did not, however, want her son involved in the solicitation of new business or exposed to the potential dangers of handling the increasingly large quantities they had begun selling. Anson was a welcome solution. The only reservation Janis and her partners had was that he appeared constantly strung out, a "speed freak." They had privately agreed to see how he might work out but would watch him carefully. If there was the slightest indication that his involvement posed any danger, they would immediately dissolve the relationship.

Janis had no amphetamines on hand the evening Anson and Don Wiley visited her house. However, she promised delivery before noon the following day. The price would be $900 per ounce.

"If it's good stuff," Wiley remarked, "that's a bargain." He told her he would need two ounces "as a sample." Then, if his friends were pleased, he'd likely be returning to purchase a pound.

The following day, Wiley and Anson met Janis and her boyfriend in a parking lot near her home, and the sale was made.

Anson's reward for bringing in the new customer was a half ounce of "speed," which he immediately used to celebrate his good fortune at having finally found an investor who would soon put him into business for himself.

The euphoric feeling, however, was short-lived.

Daily, Anson would stop in at the club only to find that Don Wiley was not there, nor had anyone seen him. It was as if he had suddenly disappeared. Complicating Anson's frustration was the fact that Janis Latham seemed to have fewer and fewer deliveries for him to make.

Instead of moving toward anticipated prosperity, Anson found himself backpedalling into a dire situation in which his own drug supply was fast drying up. Desperate, he finally confronted Janis.

Goddammit, he'd worked hard for her and her partners. He'd done them a good job for pissant pay. What the fuck was going on?

What Janis didn't tell him was that Wiley had come to her, prepared to make additional buys—but only if Anson was "cut out of their dealings." "The guy's stability worries me," Wiley explained. "He's whacked out most of the time and he carries that damn .357 with him everywhere he goes. If he's in, I'm out. It's as simple as that."

Business is business, Janis acknowledged. In her line of commerce, like all others, the customer was always right. She promised to replace Anson immediately.

Shortly thereafter Anson had called to ask that I bring his stored clothing to him. Despondent over his failure to succeed at even the lowest of professions, he had, indeed, again begun to think of disappearing into Mexico.

What he hoped to accomplish by such flight, I doubt he knew. But, in light of what was to come, I wish to God he'd gone.

IN THE EARLY DAYS of November, the fights between Anson and Annette escalated into an almost constant stream of screaming verbal bouts and physical attacks. Nearby residents complained of yelling and slamming doors in Apartment 218 at all hours of the day and night. Concerned friends of Annette whispered urgings that she get away. "Anson's crazy," one of her friends insisted, "and you're crazy if you stay with him. Take off, call the police and have him arrested . . . do whatever it takes . . . but, for Pete's sake, don't let him keep beating up on you."

Those in the apartment complex who knew Anson had, in

fact, begun going out of their way to avoid him and his quick-trigger temper. They would see him wandering about the grounds with the newspaper folded under his arm, hollow-eyed and unshaven, as if disoriented, and would quickly turn away into the safety of their apartment. Once the smiling ex-con who always had some unbelievable yet interesting story to share, he had become mean-spirited and sullen, ever ready for a confrontation. "You could see the drugs eating away at him," said one of the residents who had initially befriended Anson. "They made him mean and paranoid as hell. He became suspicious of everyone and mad at the world. At times I couldn't help but feel a little sorry for him." He too had become concerned for Annette's safety.

Still, when Anson began to talk of running to Mexico, it had been Annette who convinced him to stay. She had long ago quit using drugs. He could, too, she insisted, if he would only seek professional help. Get clean and get a job, she begged. There was in Anson something she saw that no one else could, some well-hidden good that made her cling to the unreasonable hope they might have a life together.

While all others openly voiced their fear and dislike for Anson, she chose to believe his false promises that he would turn his life around and the empty apologies for the way he'd treated her. The complexities of such a love-hate relationship defy the understanding of those viewing from an outside vantage point. She had given up trying to explain it to her puzzled friends.

After Anson promised that he would look into the possibility of entering a drug rehabilitation center she gave him a shiny new Saint Christopher medal on a gold chain. It was a token of hope, a touchstone to finally mark a new beginning.

It never came.

In short order the fighting resumed, taking on a new intensity. Despite the lack of money, Anson's drug use never slowed. Tips earned by Annette would disappear from her purse as soon as she'd fallen asleep, and within hours he would be wired, a raw nerve of energy far removed from the real world. The idea of drug rehabilitation had long since been forgotten.

On the morning of November 16, Annette woke to find Anson in the living room, sitting in front of a blaring television he'd been watching through another sleepless night.

Her anger and frustration boiled immediately, and she began yelling, demanding that he leave. She hated him, he was nothing but a common thief, a drugged-out nobody. She wished they had never let him out of prison.

In a matter of seconds Anson was on his feet, his own anger full-blown. He shoved her against the doorway. "Go back to bed and get out of my face. Just leave me the fuck alone."

She slapped him hard against the side of his face and grabbed at the band of the watch he was wearing, tearing it from his wrist and hurling it to the floor. He picked it up and threw it at her, faintly aware of a distant tinkling sound it made as it hit the wall and flew into pieces. "I'm out of here," he yelled. She was lucky, he said, that he didn't beat the shit out of her.

As he moved toward the door Annette screamed, "You sorry sonuvabitch," and raced across the room in an attempt to wrestle him to the floor. Anson shoved her away and was out into the chilly early morning, wearing only a pair of gym shorts.

For hours he walked along neighborhood streets, barefoot and shirtless, drawing puzzled stares from passersby, who were unaware of his drug-induced, anger-fueled protection against the elements. He felt nothing, saw nothing, and was accompanied only by the bitter residue of his rage.

It was still with him when he finally returned to the apartment; still with him as Annette flew into another tirade, insisting that she never wanted to see him again. If he wanted to destroy his life, go right ahead, but she was sick of hers being ruined by him.

"And yours is ruined, believe me," she said. "You're going to be headed back to prison any day now. You've really screwed it up this time."

Anson, puzzled at her statement, said nothing for a moment, waiting for her to continue.

"Your good buddy Don Wiley's a narc, a fucking DEA agent," she yelled. "He's going to put you away for a long time."

Anson grabbed her by the shoulder, pressing her against the living room wall. "How do you know?" he asked. *"How the hell do you know that?"*

"I just know."

She didn't tell him that a girlfriend who worked at the club had warned her of rumors that a drug bust would soon come down and that Anson would be among those arrested. It had been easy enough to guess that Wiley was the person who had made the cases. For several days Annette's friend had begged her to get away from Anson lest she too become involved.

Stunned by the suggestion he'd been set up by an undercover agent, that he'd allowed himself to be so easily duped, Anson slumped against a chair. The paranoia he'd so long endured suddenly grew to a new, piercing volume, throbbing at his brain, knotting his stomach. Of all the fears he had battled, that of being returned to a prison cell was the greatest. And now, if Annette was telling the truth, it could soon be realized.

For a moment he silently glared at the woman he had both loved and hated, now the smirking clarion of his worst possible nightmare.

Then, with every ounce of strength he could muster, he swung his fist into the side of her face.

When she slumped to the floor he fell on her, swept up in a mad fury, and continued delivering enraged blows, lashing out at—what? A helpless young woman he outweighed by fifty pounds? His own self-hatred? An unforgiving world that he felt had dealt him nothing but one bad hand after another?

Bleeding from her nose and mouth and on the verge of unconsciousness, Annette looked up at him. "Why don't you just kill me?" she said in a voice that was barely a whisper.

Lifting her, Anson carried her into the bedroom and roughly threw her limp body onto the bed. Cursing, he continued the vicious attack until it seemed the last drop of energy had drained from his body. Afterward, he would have no idea how long the insane rampage had lasted. It was as if all sense of time and place had been swept into a pitch-dark vacuum where there was no sound or feeling.

Drained by exhaustion and feeling suddenly dizzy, he had walked outside and sat on the concrete steps in front of the apartment. He took deep, measured gulps of the crisp fall air in an attempt to clear his head and slow the pounding inside his chest. For a moment he feared his heart might explode.

He stared down at his aching hands, where blood was already crusting on the bruised and scraped knuckles.

A half hour passed before he went back inside and slowly made his way toward the bedroom. A silence unlike anything he'd ever experienced permeated the apartment.

On the bed lay Annette's ravaged body, her once pretty, almost childlike face masked by blood, her eyes staring blankly toward the ceiling.

Still around her neck was the strand of ribbon he'd used to strangle her. Nearby was the ice pick he had plunged into her ear.

As he stood viewing the impossible horror, he had been out of prison for just seventy-six days.

IT WAS SEVERAL DAYS before I could bring myself to think of making a trip to the jail to see Anson.

In the wake of learning of Annette's death, I found myself fighting demons I'd never expected to confront. There was no place to hide from the monstrous truth, no activity that provided safe haven from a world I had only minimal ability to face. The nights brought with them an even more intense dread, filled with restless, ugly thoughts that crept into my consciousness despite all efforts to ward them off. No matter how hard I tried, images of the scene played out at the Timberline Apartments refused to stay away.

In those bleak, early morning hours when all reason and judgment disappear and the quiet magnifies the smallest things into horror story proportions, I found myself wishing that it had been me whom Anson had killed.

Questions haunted me: What could I have done to prevent this irreparable tragedy? Had my not allowing him to return home upon his release been a decision that had set this terrible scenario in motion? Why hadn't I stayed in closer touch and been more demanding that Anson seek help? How could a member of my own family have been a party to so many things—drugs, domestic violence, and now murder—that I could not possibly forgive? I thought often of Annette's family, wanting to contact them, yet at a complete loss for the words that might assure them that their grief was not being ignored.

Pat summoned supportive strengths I'm sure she had never anticipated a need for, and friends stopped by for brief, awkward visits. Though they never really knew what to say, their missions were clearly fueled by the best of intentions.

Ironically, the arrival of two police officers is what, to this day, I most vividly remember and appreciate.

While doing my research for the book on the slain undercover agent, I had come to know Midlothian Police Chief Roy Vaughn and Lieutenant Billy Fowler quite well. Our relationship had rapidly developed well beyond that of writer and subject, flowering into genuine friendship. Both longtime veterans of the Dallas Police Department, retirement had suited neither, and they had chosen to continue their law enforcement careers in the slow-paced atmosphere of the rural community they watched over. Then the serenity of their lives had been jolted by the murder of the young undercover officer whom Vaughn had hired and Fowler had trained.

I was, at first, amazed at how deeply affected both had been by the senseless tragedy. Strong men who had spent much of their adult lives dealing with the worst of social horrors, tears came freely when they spoke of the untimely death of the young man both had felt fatherly responsibility for.

Their tragedy had brought us together. And on the night after Anson's arrest, it was mine that had drawn them to me.

I was hardly the first relative of a murderer they had spoken to during their careers, and they were quick to share their experiences and insight.

"Right now," Fowler said, "you're feeling a lot more guilt than you should. You're looking for someone to blame, anyone other than your boy, and you're the most convenient target. Unless I'm mistaken, you're beating up on yourself pretty good right now. It's a natural reaction, but the fact is you shouldn't be doing it. You *aren't* to blame for what happened. That's the most important thing to remember right now. To get through this, you've got to convince yourself of that."

He offered another warning: "Don't rush out and hire a lawyer to defend him. It'll run into thousands of dollars before you realize what's hit you. Let the courts take care of it. They'll appoint someone as qualified as you could afford to hire. I've seen families use up their life savings, sell their homes, and borrow until they couldn't anymore, for nothing. It ruined them. The truth is, there's not a lot you can do to help your son. So think about those you can do something for."

Vaughn voiced his agreement. "There are," he added, "a lot of people—a lot of your friends—who are looking at your situation right now and feel badly for you. They aren't holding you responsible. Hell, if they've got kids themselves they're saying, 'There but for the grace of God . . .' Nobody with a lick of sense is blaming you. So don't blame yourself."

It was a task easier said than accomplished. It would take time.

But, if nothing else, their visit convinced me that hiding away, brooding in solitude, would serve only as a useless, even cowardly, exercise. People knew what had happened. They'd read the papers, listened to newscasts, talked among themselves, and formed whatever opinions they would.

Pat seemed both surprised and relieved when, just days after Anson's arrest, I showered and dressed to go out to the offices of the Dallas Cowboys. Among the part-time responsibilities I'd taken on since leaving the *Dallas Morning News* was the weekly editing of the tabloid newspaper published by the club. It was basically a one-man task, requiring a long day and night of editing copy provided by other freelance writers, selecting photographs to be used, doing page layouts, and preparing assignments for the next week's issue.

As I arrived, the first person I encountered in the hallway was Doug Todd, the affable, always joking director of team publicity. He walked quickly toward me, a look of genuine concern on his face. "What the hell are you doing here?"

I borrowed from his own repertoire of quick replies, choosing one he himself had stolen years earlier from a happy-go-lucky Cowboys quarterback named Don Meredith. "Everybody's got to be somewhere," I answered.

I went about my duties in rote, self-absorbed fashion, keenly aware that those around me were at a loss for what to say. Gracefully, those who did stop by my desk opted for the safety and comfort of brief, measured small talk. For the most part, silence ran through my day as if it guarded a secret no one wished to hear.

It was late in the evening when I finally left for home. If nothing else, I'd proven to myself that I remained functional. It was a start.

My next venture, however, would not be so easy.

A NIGHT VISIT to the Lew Sterrett Justice Center—Dallas County's main jail—offers a dreaded encounter with all manner of social misery. Lines of cheerless faces—predominantly black—wind toward a bank of lobby windows to deposit small amounts of money into the accounts of incarcerated friends and loved ones. Across the stark, fluorescent-lit foyer, weary lawyers arrange bail for clients whose misdeeds have extended their workday far past the dinner hour. Along the walls, women in their late teens or early twenties, with tired faces and accompanied by restless, bewildered children, sit and wait patiently for the release of husbands and boyfriends. The acrid smells of vending machine coffee, cheap perfumes, and a solitary custodian's bucket of cleaning ammonia added to the assault on the senses. Though a relatively new facility, the building has about it a ground-in griminess that the most miraculous of cleansing agents will never cure. It is dirty, depressing, and echoes with the pain of those forced to frequent it.

THE ROUTINE had not changed. The waiting game began with a walk down the concrete hallway in the back of the building, ending at a small table where a bored deputy sat, handing out visiting slips to be filled out. In a box were half a dozen stubs of pencils for those who had not brought their own.

Once he checked the information I'd written and studied my driver's license for what seemed like an inordinate amount of time, he flipped idly through his computer printout of inmates and their location.

"Step back and wait until your name is called," the deputy said without bothering even to look up from his paperwork.

A half hour passed before I was called to the elevator leading up to the cell blocks, leaving behind a still-growing crowd of disgruntled visitors who lined the hallway, waiting to hear their names called.

The waiting continued as I was directed into a small booth in which a plastic chair faced a window that looked into a mirror image of the tiny, airless room where I sat. On both walls were the black telephone receivers through which we would communicate.

Minutes passed like hours as I waited for them to escort Anson to the opposite side of the window, wondering what I could say, what to expect. Breathing became difficult, as if no amount of effort would allow me to swallow a satisfactory amount of air into my lungs.

The abrupt pneumatic sound of the door opening from the jail side of the booth jolted me from my thoughts, and I felt a quick rush of anxiety as I tried with little success to strike a casual pose.

Taking a seat across from me was a wasted stranger. Dressed in the oversize orange jumpsuit issued all inmates charged with murder, Anson looked across at me through lifeless eyes, nodding a greeting as he reached for his phone.

"I didn't think you would come this time," he said. There was a brittle tone to his voice I'd never before heard.

My eyes burned as I forced back tears. What to say? How to play this difficult part that I had never prepared for? Did I remind him that I'd always come? How many times? How many jails in how many years in how many cities? Dammit, hadn't I always been there for him, even when he had done his best to push me away?

It was several seconds before I responded. "You're still my son."

He put his head down and stared at the concrete floor.

"You want to talk about it?"

"Not really," he said. "I did it. I'd give anything in the world if I could change it . . . but I can't." He'd already given a full confession, he said, and would not ask for a trial. His court-appointed attorney had told him to expect to be sentenced to sixty years if he simply pled guilty. "But that's what I'm going to do," he added. "I'm going to go back where I belong."

An unsettling thought raced through my mind. The decision he spoke of was, I realized, what I had wanted to hear. The thought that some inventive attorney might convince a jury to acquit Anson violated everything I believed in. Over the years I had become increasingly skeptical of the real fairness of the judicial system, watching as too many defense lawyers played nothing more than high-priced games in an effort to get clients, regardless of how despicable their acts, set free. Though admittedly simplistic, I had continued to hold to my Baptist upbringing belief that a criminal act merited punishment. My own son was no exception.

"You know there's not much I can do . . ."

Anson raised a hand and pressed it to the glass. "Dad, I don't expect you to do anything. *I don't want* you to do anything. This time neither of us can."

He was silent for a minute, as though searching for words that were lost. His eyes, ringed in dark circles, moistened. "I loved her," he finally said. "I loved her . . . but I treated her so badly . . . and then I killed her. It doesn't make much sense, does it?"

I shook my head. "No, it doesn't."

We talked for a few more minutes, neither really saying much. I asked if he was getting any rest, eating anything, and told him I would mail him some books and see that he had commissary money. And that I would be back to visit again.

As I stood, preparing to leave, he motioned toward the receiver I'd already replaced, signaling for me to pick it back up. "I've got a favor to ask," he said.

"What's that?"

"They've got my clothes and stuff down in the property room. In the pocket of my pants there's a Saint Christopher medal on a gold chain. Annette gave it to me on my birthday. I've talked to the guard and he says he'll get it to me if someone brings it up here. I'd really like to have it."

I promised him I would do so as a jailer appeared at his door to escort him back to his cell.

At that moment, however, I had the feeling that there was nothing more important than getting out of the building as quickly as possible, away from the bars and clanging doors and the muffled, faraway voices—my son's mixed somewhere among them—of those warehoused behind them.

Once back on the main floor, I fought the strong urge to break into a run toward the door and into the fresh night air, to distance myself from something I knew had been lost forever.

Instead, I sought out the property room and after lengthy pleading was given the dime-size medal Anson had requested. Taking the elevator back to the floor where he was being held, I found a guard who promised to see that it would be delivered to my son.

Later, as I walked toward the parking lot, our brief conversation replaying through my mind, an unwelcome but familiar companion joined me—a feeling I had lived with for years. It was a dark, insidious enemy I had privately faced, never really understanding its origin or purpose. As always, it came swiftly, without warning, causing my stomach to knot into sudden, painful spasms, my chest to tighten. A sudden coldness would sweep through my body.

I had given it a variety of aliases, ranging from anger to depression, but the enemy's true name was fear. Stark, gripping fear, which I had never fully understood or known how to fight against. It was not the kind of apprehension a soldier must feel in wartime. Nor was it akin to the terror that accompanies some invisible threat to one's well-being. The man walking down a dark alley in a bad part of town would not understand what I'd been so unsuccessful at defining. Neither would the lost child or the business tycoon whose financial empire had suddenly crumbled. My fear had always seemed somehow special, beyond explanation's reach.

But in that early winter darkness, accompanied only by the quick, visible bursts my breathing made against the chilled air, the dreaded enemy finally identified itself. Why it chose that moment, I have no idea, but the sudden understanding came mockingly and was so fundamental in nature that I paused to wonder why I had not grasped it long before.

My fear was not of personal harm or professional ruin or even my own time to die. Mine was the fear of things over which I had no control, things that, regardless of how mightily I might try, I could neither prevent nor change.

Having finally seen its face, I felt the gentle touch of relief and the slow-arriving hint of something I knew would eventually build to a new confidence. Somewhere in the still-faint distance loomed the possible recovery of a lost belief in self and a world again righted.

The battle, I knew, would be neither short nor easy. In all likelihood, it would be ongoing for as long as mind and memory continued to function.

I drove toward home, leaving behind one shattered life, vowing to rebuild the fragile pieces of my own.

Epilogue

FIVE YEARS HAVE PASSED since that early spring when I sat in a small, almost empty Dallas court-room and listened as my son pled guilty to murder. The proceedings were mercifully short, lasting no more than ten minutes. I was relieved to see that the brief flurry of interest the media had shown in the case had disappeared. No reporters stood by, taking notes and forming questions to which I still had no wish to respond.

As he was led away, back to the jail cell he would occupy until he was transferred to prison, Anson stopped briefly and turned to where Pat and I sat, the lone visitors in the courtroom. I could not hear him but was able to read his words. "Thanks for being here," he said.

With that a part of our lives ended.

Anson's shattered future now promised nothing more than year after year of prison life's mind-numbing monotony. How much chess and how many card games could one play, how many books could one read, how much television watching would it take to pass the time of each endless day?

He would be almost forty-five years old before being again eligible for parole. It was a lifetime away, too far in the distance even to contemplate, so out of reach that it would not even serve as hope to hold to in the dark nights and long days to come.

As Pat and I drove from the courthouse that day, we rode in silence much of the way. "He looked so small," she finally said. "I know it sounds odd, but all I could think of as he was standing there in front of the judge was how small he looked. It was like looking at someone I'd never seen before."

She leaned toward me, gently placing her hand on my shoulder. "Are you going to be okay?"

I nodded, lacking words to explain to her the strange mixture of thoughts racing through my mind. In a way, Annette's was not the only tragic, untimely death that had occurred. With his horrible crime, Anson too had stepped over into that netherworld where all things good rot and die. The son I had once known, loved, and so long agonized over was gone.

Upon our arrival home we stood in the yard for a time, savoring the fresh air of the real world, inhaling the sweet fragrance of late-blooming honeysuckle that floated on the soft breeze and watched as the neighborhood squirrels played games of chase through the trees.

"I was proud of him," I said, thinking aloud.

The puzzled look on my wife's face begged an explanation.

"What Anson did today was something he's not been able to do most of his life, something I'd lost hope of ever seeing again. He finally took responsibility for his actions. There was no lying, no effort to place the blame on someone or something else. He admitted his guilt and accepted his punishment."

There was, I knew, a disturbing irony woven into my observation. Why had it taken the worst of all possible situations to bring out what I judged the best in my son?

S L O W L Y , life began to regain a sense of normalcy. The depression that had haunted me began to dissipate only after I did something I'd sworn never to do. Though at first skeptical, I finally sought counseling, sharing locked-away feelings with a total stranger for the first time in my life. The antidepressant he prescribed brought sweet, easy sleep for the first time in weeks.

Pat pulled me to midafternoon movies and long evening walks along the same course we'd traveled during the aftermath of her bout with cancer. I could not help but marvel at the quiet reversal of roles. Now it was she who chattered optimistically of days to come, talking of anything and everything except the one thing that weighed so heavily on both our minds. Friends—some, I suspect, secretly prompted by calls from my wife—phoned with invitations for lunch. As the Christmas season neared, our home took on a festive warmth beyond any that Pat had ever before created. This, she announced, was the year we finally dressed the front yard and ordered me to the task. Soon, passersby saw the cheerful nighttime twinkle of holiday lights, blinking a signal that all was well in the Stowers house. My dad, a bass fisherman with few peers, phoned to remind me that the big ones always bit in winter weather and insisted that I visit for a few days.

And I began to work again, trying to focus on the realities of deadlines and bills that demanded payment.

To my surprise a time eventually came when thoughts of Anson were so obscured that several days might pass without my dwelling on his fate. Among the most remarkable gifts God had given man, I was learning, were resiliency and a capability to cope and continue on.

For years I had tried, with precious little success, to do what all loving fathers attempt. But no amount of support or discipline, advice or warning, had diverted Anson from his course. Nothing I did properly elevated his ego or convinced him of the world's goodness. I had never been able to share with him the treasured gift of well-being.

There is, at such times, a natural inclination to seek a place for blame. Some willfully, even eagerly, shoulder it, wearing it like a self-inflicted scarlet letter signaling their failure. Others are quick to disavow all responsibility and accountability. I never knew what attitude to embrace as uncertain feelings changed and shifted like a summer wind.

It was Pat who issued a warning that finally caught my attention. "If you let it, this will destroy you just as surely as it has Anson. And what would that accomplish except to compound the tragedies that have already occurred? You've got other people who need and want your concern. You've got another son who loves you and wants more than anything else in the world to please you and make you proud. My boys think the world of you. And, God knows, I need you.

"Let it go," she said. "What has happened is not your fault."

I wanted so to believe her and to heed her advice. Too, I hoped for her observations to be something more than that of a loving, concerned wife offering solace.

"Let me ask you something," she continued. "In looking back at your relationship with Anson, the way you raised him, the things you said and did and tried to do, what would you have done differently? If you could go back and do it all over, what changes would you have made?"

It was a question I'd often asked myself, one, in fact, I had pondered with the arrival of each new crisis that had occurred over the years. Yet, for some reason, I had never formed a satisfactory answer. But now, when posed by someone else, it seemed different, finally demanding an honest answer.

"I really don't know," I said. "The fact is, I'd probably do it just the same because, at the time, it seemed right. If there were better ways, I didn't see them. And even with the advantage of hindsight, I still can't. The truth is, there are few things I'd likely be able to do much better if given a second chance."

"So," she said, "you did your best." she replied. "That's all anyone—you included—can possibly do."

A N D S O I slowly retreated to a safe distance from all that had occurred, staking claim to a more comfortable middle ground. The time had come to cease assuming blame for the sins of my son. On the other hand, the idea of trying suddenly and completely to shut him from my life, to try and move ahead without so much as an acknowledgment that he still existed, was out of the question. There was no crime so great that it could erase the fact he was still in my heart and mind.

In truth, the judicial system had provided me with a long-sought respite as well as an avenue of resolve. By decree of the court, any relationship Anson and I might have for years to come would be one conducted only at arm's length. Any direction I might have lent to his life was now in the hands of the criminal justice system.

INSTEAD, I watched as Ashley eagerly tested the first adventures of manhood. Following graduation from high school he was determined to move to Southern California. His motivation was twofold: There, in the land of sunny beaches, was the promise of excitement, opportunity, and the independence he was eager to experience. It was also where his high school girlfriend and her family were now living.

For a time I had argued for college or enrollment in some kind of trade school, maybe even a stint in the military, but he made it clear that higher education held no more immediate attraction than wearing a uniform. He wanted to travel to the West Coast, find a job, and spend some time determining what he wanted to do with the remainder of his life.

Secretly, I envied his adventurous spirit.

In time, he had settled in California, happily reunited with his girlfriend, and was working as a waiter in a popular restaurant in the Los Angeles suburbs.

Over the years he had spoken of Anson less and less, only mentioning receipt of a letter, a piece of his brother's artwork, or an occasional phone conversation. He had, with no advice from me, determined his own manner of dealing with his brother's fate. There was nothing he could do that would alter the state of Anson's affairs, so he had opted to focus his energies elsewhere, concentrating on his own efforts to find his place in adult society.

Which was, I felt, a healthy approach. Far removed from the site of old hurts and troublesome memories, he could focus on building his own life.

On trips to the West Coast for the Cowboys' annual training camp or occasional book promotions, I visited him and was delighted by the growing maturity I saw. If he privately wrestled with questions about his brother's misspent life, he did not share them with me. And I felt it best to leave it that way. What I saw was what every parent hopes for: a young man taking control of his own life, delighting in the daily challenges and experiences one faces when finally freed of old bonds.

Which is not to say there haven't been times when the troubling past has visited.

On a summer weekend in 1990, Pat took an anxious call from Ashley. (As so often seems the case, I was out of town on some now-forgotten writing assignment.) He had been at work one evening when his roommate phoned from the apartment with disturbing news.

"He said that Anson had called and said he was planning an escape from prison and would be seeing me in a few days," Ashley, obviously unnerved, explained. "What should I do?"

Pat told him she would get in touch with me.

As I listened to what she had to say my mind raced. What in hell's name was Anson thinking? What could I do to abort such an absurd plan? Had he really been serious, or just attempting a very unfunny joke? Unfortunately, his history of escapes, first from the juvenile detention facility in Dallas, then the jail in Louisiana, forced me to lend a measure of credence to the possibility that he did, in fact, plan to try an escape.

Telling Pat I was on my way home, I asked that she phone Billy Fowler, the Midlothian police lieutenant with whom I'd become friends during the writing of *Innocence Lost*. "Explain to him what's happened and ask what he thinks should be done. I know that all the prison phone calls are taped, so maybe he can get someone there to check and find out what was actually said."

I then called Ashley in an attempt to persuade him not to worry.

By the time I arrived home, the situation had been resolved. After receiving Fowler's call, prison officials had immediately placed Anson in an isolation cell while they searched for a recording of the conversation. Then had come another call from Ashley. "After I got home," he said, "my roommate admitted that he'd made it all up. He says he just did it as a joke. Anson did call, but he just shot the breeze. He didn't say anything about trying to escape." There was a welcome sound of relief in his voice.

Then his roommate came on the phone, a nice young man whom Ashley had earlier brought to Texas for a visit. I'd liked him and had enjoyed having him as a guest. Now, however, I had no interest in his apology. "You scared the hell out of a lot of people," I charged. "Ashley, my wife, me. And because of your stupid little stunt, Anson, whose life isn't exactly a bed of roses on the best of days, is sitting in solitary confinement until the mess you've created can be sorted out."

"I'm sorry," he replied.

Furious, I slammed down the phone.

It was but another example of the effect Anson had on our lives, even though far removed.

I STOPPED MAKING VISITS to prison. For a time the urge to make my way back into the gray maze and see him continued to beckon, but I chose to ignore it. I invented excuses until finally they ran out. Weeks ran into months, months into years.

We corresponded and spoke occasionally by phone. I routinely mailed small amounts of money so that he might visit the commissary for tobacco and personal items. And I sent him books—spy novels, science fiction, mysteries—and we exchanged greeting cards on holidays, mine generally carrying some humorous message, his self-drawn in ink or colored pencils.

It was as close as I chose to get. A letter in which he described the dismal aspects of prison was one thing; seeing it firsthand was something else. Hearing him tell me of some fight he'd gotten into with a fellow inmate was less painful than viewing the bruises.

By maintaining a comfortable distance, I had decided, I could hold to the new order that was emerging in my own life.

Research for a magazine article caused me to be in the Dallas office of nationally known forensic psychiatrist Dr. James Grigson. A lanky, southern gentleman whose charm and good nature dramatically contradicts the moniker given him by the media, Grigson had testified in more than 2,000 criminal cases during his controversial career. On 150 occasions he's taken the witness stand to aid prosecutors in convincing juries that offenders in capital murder cases deserved the death penalty. Thus the nickname, "Dr. Death."

Once our interview was completed we adjourned to a nearby restaurant for lunch, and during the course of our mealtime conversation, I was mildly surprised when he inquired about Anson. "You know," he said, "that I spoke with him while he was in jail."

During those hectic days immediately following Annette's death and Anson's arrest, much had escaped my attention—including the fact the district attorney's office had sought Grigson's help in determining my son's mental state. The purpose of his visit had been to determine if Anson was, in fact, mentally stable enough to waive all rights to a trial and simply plead guilty to his crime.

"I liked him," Grigson said.

Aware of the doctor-patient privilege that protects the confidentiality of such conversations, I fought against a sudden urge to barrage the man seated across from me with questions. Just a few feet away was someone, I knew, who might hold answers that had eluded me for years, yet a code of ethics prevented him from divulging any secrets Anson might have shared with him. Our conversation quickly moved to safer ground.

It was only as we lingered over coffee that Dr. Grigson, perhaps sensing my need to know something, anything, that might shed light on my son's frame of mind, briefly returned to the subject.

"One of the things I do when I speak to people in jail," he said, "is to ask them about their relationship with their families. Since I've known you for some time, I was particularly interested in how your boy felt about you and the relationship the two of you have had."

I could feel my heart pounding as I anxiously awaited the answer I knew was coming.

"Your son," Dr. Grigson said in a voice so soft and soothing that it was almost hypnotic, "loves you very much. He told me, in fact, that he considers you his best friend."

With that he pled the need to return to work. He'd said all he was going to on the subject.

For weeks Dr. Grigson's words lingered in my thoughts like some treasured old song. Why, I wondered, would Anson tell a complete stranger things he'd never told me? What impenetrable barrier existed between us that made it so difficult to share such feelings with me?

In the days that followed, the idea for this book slowly began to form. But not without old reservations. I wondered, had enough time passed, enough healing and maturing, to make another run at the truth worthwhile? Or was it so hidden away, so painfully guarded, that no amount of effort would allow it to surface?

Finally, late one night in the summer of 1993, I wrote to Anson, proposing a series of visits during which we might look back on our lives together in an honest, no-holds-barred manner. In anticipation of a question I knew he would have, I ended the letter with an attempt at explanation: "I know you are asking yourself why, after all these years, I am proposing such a project. The answer is neither simple nor one I'm sure I can satisfactorily offer. But if there is some understanding to be reached I think it might benefit us both."

A few days later I received a reply. "I agree," Anson wrote in his familiar, flowery handwriting. "Let's do it."

THE SCENES AND ROUTINE were familiar. Inside the stark white visitors' lobby people awaited the moment they would be ushered inside to visit friends and loved ones. Some sat silently, anxiously clutching the form they had earlier filled out. Others passed the time reading newspapers or paperbacks, which they would be required to store in the small metal lockers lining one wall before entering the prison yard. As always, those who had come to visit were mostly female—mothers, wives, and girlfriends—and I found myself smiling at the nervous primping that took place around me. Some had small children in tow, calming them with treats from nearby vending machines. Most of them were veterans of previous visits and had clear plastic sandwich bags filled with the change they would be allowed to carry inside with them to purchase cigarettes, soft drinks, and snacks. The atmosphere, as always, was tense, much like that of a late-night hospital waiting room.

As I leaned against the wall, waiting to hear my name called, I read over the questionnaire a female jailer had routinely requested that each visitor fill out. In addition to my name and address, driver's license number, and the prisoner I wished to visit, there was an odd variety of other queries: Had I ever been convicted of a felony? Ever done time? What was my relation to person I wished to visit? Did I remember to lock my car before entering the building?

As the form requested, I had deposited my ring, billfold, a set of nail clippers, and car keys in one of the lockers. I would enter the prison yard with only the clothes that were on my back and my bag filled with five dollars' worth of nickels, dimes, and quarters.

Once my name was called and my papers read and approved, I entered a locked hallway where a guard instructed me to remove my shoes, turn my pockets inside out, and walk slowly through a metal detector. I was then patted down and required to open my mouth and lift my tongue so that a penlight search could determine if I was attempting to smuggle anything in.

Then, finally, there was the thud of hydraulic machinery that opened the door leading out to the miniworld of the prison yard visitation area. There were a dozen or so wooden picnic tables, a few benches, and a swing set to occupy the children. A paved strip, carefully marked, ran the fifty-yard length of the area, providing the opportunity for those tired of sitting to walk back and forth in a slow promenade with no destination.

Everywhere, eager eyes awaited the first glimpse of husbands, lovers, fathers—and sons—released into the visiting yard.

There is always that anxious moment that precedes such meetings. What to say? Who speaks first? Handshake or hug?

DRESSED IN JEANS, a dark T-shirt, and running shoes, Anson was trim and fit. He had obviously been spending his time in the exercise yard wisely. There was a welcoming smile on his face as he approached that immediately wiped away all apprehension I had been feeling about the trip.

It was good to see him.

The heat of the early afternoon sun was tempered by a comforting breeze, and we hurriedly claimed a spot on one of the benches. The conversation at first was hesitant, akin to the small talk made by strangers getting acquainted. And for a time I was a voyeur in a strange world, keenly aware of my surroundings: the stern-faced guards who silently stood watch, the passionate embraces of men and women sitting nearby, the children at play.

It was Anson, responding to a question about his health, who moved the conversation toward a more serious topic. "Dad," he said, "I've been clean for almost two years."

His last encounter with drugs had come, he recalled, when his cell mate's girlfriend had smuggled a small bag of heroin in to him. "He shared it with me, and for about a week afterward I was sick as a dog. I vomited until I thought I'd turn inside out. After that, I just decided it wasn't worth it anymore.

"Not long ago, a guy owed me thirty dollars I'd won off him playing pinochle. He tried to pay me off with a bag of heroin, and I told him I didn't want it. But he insisted, saying he didn't have any money. So, I figured what the hell, and took it. Later, I just gave it to another guy. He wanted to know how much he owed me, and I told him 'nothing.'

"People still offer me stuff now and then," he continued, "but I just tell them I'm not interested. Some of them find it a little strange, I think—not many guys around here turn down a chance to get high and forget their troubles for a while—but nobody really hassles me about it.

"I like the fact that I feel better physically than I have in a long time."

I was pleased to hear a ring of sincerity to what he was saying. Though he stopped short of saying as much, turning away from drugs was an accomplishment for which he felt obvious and justifiable pride. For someone who had once sampled from the street dealers' entire menu, it was no small victory.

"And," he continued, "a lot of the anger I've been carrying around for so much of my life is gone. Well, maybe not really *gone*, but under better control. I've spent a lot of time by myself in the last couple of years, sitting in the hole for fighting or doing tattooing, stuff like that. It has given me the opportunity to do a lot of thinking.

"I've still got a temper—I don't guess that will ever change—but my patience has improved. Hell, maybe I've just grown up some and come to the realization that there are things that really aren't worth getting into a fight over. Maybe I've finally reached the point where I don't want to deal with the hassle anymore."

In the days that followed he talked even more freely of things past and present, displaying a candor I frankly had not expected. Finally, we were no longer talking as father and son, man and child, but as adults no longer bound by the roles we'd each so long played. We teased each other's memories, shared new feelings, sorted out fact from fantasy and truths from old lies. There was far more laughter than I had dared expect.

Those initial conversations—and the many that would follow—breathed the life into this project, giving it real purpose and direction.

And while there are still things beyond my own futile attempts at comprehension that will forever trouble me, a measure of inner peace has resulted from the pursuit. It is my sincere hope that Anson can say the same.

At the very least, it has been a worthwhile learning experience.

PERHAPS ALL THIS would have made more sense had I not cared, if Anson had been abused and deprived in his younger days, cast away without love or guidance. Those, however, are convenient explanations that are not available. Somewhere, somehow, we simply took paths that, over the years, led us further and further apart.

If nothing else, I've finally learned that there are questions for which there are no satisfactory responses. To ask them is natural, even a driven need, but the only real wisdom that can result is an acceptance that they, like even the most desperate prayers, may never be answered. Perhaps in the grand scheme of things there are things not meant to be fully explained or completely understood.

There is a photograph, slightly out of focus and not framed by a professional's eye, that I look to now and then for assurance that there were, in fact, good times. It has become my link to a treasured bygone moment. In it, a smiling, young Anson hugs Ginger, the Shetland pony that became part of our family in those long-ago days back in Comfort. There is about the picture a warm, sweet innocence only the young ever really know.

The boy is happy and loving, far too carefree to ponder the hardships of an adult world, too filled with wonder to be concerned with the dark clouds of the future.

Only recently did I retrieve it from the box where mementos from another time had been hidden away and place it in a frame that now sits on my desk. It is faded, like the memories it evokes, but there is a genuine comfort in having it nearby.

There comes a time, in matters of the heart, when one must set aside the anger and disappointments and seek warmth that drives away the cold and, finally, begins to soften the bad with good.

Acknowledgments

THERE ARE THOSE who made important and much-appreciated contributions to this book long before I even knew I would write it. Some, for private reasons, wish to remain anonymous. Understand, though, that the omission of their names in no way lessens my gratitude for their help and insight.

In a manner of speaking, this book is as much Anson's as it is mine. Frankly, had he not agreed that it was a worthy endeavor, I would never have undertaken it. So, Son, I thank you first and offer the sincere hope that this exploration benefited you as it did me.

The encouragement of my wife, Pat, was the fuel that drove the project to completion, and it came as no small comfort to know that my son Ashley deemed the idea a good one and blessed it with his support.

For jogging my memory and providing needed help at vital times, I'm indebted to the Reverend Dean Pratt, Mike Barclay, Phil Hambrick, Roy Vaughn, Billy Fowler, Dr. Mark Unterburg, Clara Roark, Dr. James Grigson, Shawna Sanders, Sheila Jordan, Sharon Valenti, Beverly Deignan, Ronald Duval, Linda Martin, Brad Lollar, and Arch McColl III.

And, once more, Janet Wilkens Manus took the duties of literary agent above and beyond. Thanks also to Brian DeFiore for the encouragement, enthusiasm, and patience.

I would be remiss if I did not mention the name of colleague Skip Hollandsworth, a fine *Texas Monthly* writer who, without even knowing it, pushed me toward the decision to do this book. "It's the one," he said almost offhandedly one day, "that everyone who knows you is waiting for you to write."

Too, be aware that certain names of people mentioned have been changed in the interest of their privacy.

A final thought: As mentioned elsewhere, my work has placed me in the company of a number of people who have been the victims of family tragedies, and I've watched in admiration the manner in which they dealt with their sorrows and angers and marveled at their remarkable courage and strength of will. Their names are: Nancy Wiser, Rod Montgomery, Jan and Robert Thompson, Richard Franks, Sandra Sadler, Dr. Peter Gailiunas, Henry and Angela Agostinelli, Mark and Paula Donahue, Don and Shirley Moore, David and Sheryl Zanolini, and Mark and Sherry Prine. I thank each for friendship so willingly given and a special brand of strength I've borrowed from more often than any of them know.

—Carlton Stowers

About the Author

C ARLTON STOWERS is the author of more than two dozen nonfiction books, including the Edgar Award–winning *Careless Whispers,* the Pulitzer Prize–nominated *Innocence Lost,* and *Open Secrets.* He has also written two books for children—*A Hero Named George* and *Hard Lessons*—which are being used by elementary schools as part of their drug and gang prevention programs. He and his wife live in Cedar Hill, Texas.